Silent Stones

Mark O'Sullivan is the acclaimed and award-winning author of the bestselling *Melody for Nora* (winner of the 1995 Bisto Book Eilís Dillon Memorial Award, short-listed for the 1995 Reading Association of Ireland Award, selected as a White Raven book by international librarians); *Wash-Basin Street Blues*, also a bestseller; *More Than a Match*; *White Lies*, also selected as a White Raven book; and *Angels Without Wings* (all published by Wolfhound Press). Four of his novels have been nominated for the Bisto Book of the Year Award, and his work has been translated into six languages. Mark lives in Thurles with his wife and two daughters.

For Joan, Jane and Ruth

ALSO BY MARK O'SULLIVAN

Melody for Nora

Wash-Basin Street Blues

More Than a Match

Angels Without Wings

White Lies

Silent Stones

Mark O'Sullivan

WOLFHOUND PRESS

First published in 1999 by
Wolfhound Press Ltd
68 Mountjoy Square
Dublin 1, Ireland
Tel: (353-1) 874 0354
Fax: (353-1) 872 0207

The Arts Council
An Chomhairle Ealaíon
Wolfhound Press receives financial assistance from The Arts Council/An Chomhairle Ealaíon, Dublin, Ireland.

British Library Cataloguing in Publication Data
A catalogue record for this book is available from the British Library.

ISBN 0-86327-722-5

10 9 8 7 6 5 4 3 2 1

Cover illustration: The Slide File, Dublin
Cover Design: Slick Fish Design, Dublin
Typesetting: Wolfhound Press
Printed and bound by The Guernsey Press Co., Guernsey, Channel Islands

Chapter 1

'We'll have to shoot him,' Eamon Wade said, poking at the open fire in the farmhouse kitchen.

In the old wicker basket by the hearth, Rusty, the red setter, whined and moaned. The covering blanket rose and fluttered and fell with every spasm of pain. From the corner of the dog's mouth spewed a thick foam smelling of rotted grass. Robby wiped it away with a corner of the blanket.

'He'll make it,' he told his great-uncle. But the red setter's body contracted, stiffened like a sail whipped by wind. Long seconds passed before the taut muscles slackened again.

'Didn't I tell you what the vet said?' Eamon insisted. 'He wanted to put him down.'

'Rusty's strong. He's always been strong.'

'Robby, I know when a dog is finished. I've been around them all my life. And that one is finished.'

'Tomorrow, maybe ....'

Standing up stiffly, Eamon picked up the walking-stick he'd fashioned for himself after his left leg had been shattered, sixteen years before, in the Fermanagh ambush. The stick, old as Robby himself, had a big rough knot for a handle, polished to a sculpted knuckle by constant use. Eamon limped across to the door which led to the farmyard. His cheeks were flushed, but not from the heat of the fire. The unhealthily high colour had been there for weeks — ever since Eamon's old Republican comrade, Razor McCabe, had hit the headlines again by kidnapping a rich businessman and then escaping capture when the a rich businessman and then escaping capture when the victim had been rescued by the gardaí.

'I'm not listening to him howling all night again,' Eamon said. 'I'll get the gun from the barn. Bring him up to the Stone Field and I'll do the job.'

Robby waited until Eamon had stepped out into the yard before muttering, 'Don't miss with the first shot, like you did above in Fermanagh.'

Back in the doorway, Eamon cast a lowering shadow over Robby and the dying dog. Like all the Wades of Cloghercree, he was over six feet tall. Walking with a stick had hunched his body, but when he drew his shoulders back, the illusion of strength reappeared, if only fleetingly.

'What was that you said?' he asked.

'I said ....' Robby hesitated, then drew himself up so that his eyes were level with his great-uncle's. 'I said I'd prefer to do it myself.'

'Are you sure?' Eamon's tone softened, but only briefly. 'Has to be done. He didn't get poisoned for nothing, you know. He must've been killing sheep.'

'Rusty is no killer.'

'Well, killer or not, he'll be better off dead now.'

'I'll need a shovel,' Robby snapped.

'There's one in the ditch up near the Stone Field gate, I think. I was clearing out that drain for the winter. Must finish it one of these days.'

Returning to his chair, Eamon took up his relentless fire-poking again. For all his efforts, the ancient, thick-walled house remained icily cold even on summer days as warm as this one.

Robby uncovered the dog and lifted him up. The weight of pain, and perhaps the instinctive knowledge of his fate, made Rusty a heavier burden than Robby had expected. Eamon looked disinterestedly at the dog. Then the puttering flames drew his attention away to another place, another time.

'I'll head up to the cemetery while you're gone,' he said.

Robby made no answer. He didn't visit his father's grave any longer; he hadn't for almost a year. The precise date of that last visit was etched in his memory. Thursday, 16 August, a grey morning at the tail end of a relentlessly grey summer. Three days later, a car bomb in Omagh had taken the lives of twenty-nine people — thirty-one, Robby always insisted, remembering the unborn twins who had died in their mother's womb. Men, women and children had been slaughtered and maimed, and to Robby it was as if his own long-dead father had driven the car into the heart of that town. All the doubts that had begun to fester in his mind had found their focus then.

Shot dead six months before Robby was born, Sean Wade had never been more than a figure of myth to his son. Cúchulain, Finn McCool, seemed hardly less remote than that nineteen-year-old Republican martyr. The closest Robby ever came to him was in the nightmare that returned so often to disturb his sleep.

Robby's mother, before she went and married Liam O'Neill, had often spoken of her carefree teenage years with Sean. She might as well have been speaking of some stranger. All through his childhood, it was the gun-toting freedom fighter Robby had chosen to imagine as he weeded the grave in the nearby cemetery — not the young rocker who had idolised Phil Lynott and played hurling with the county minor team and had his sights set on university and a career in engineering. Now Robby left the grave for Eamon to keep.

Struggling under Rusty's weight, he watched his great-uncle. At fifty-eight, Eamon had made an old man of himself. His hair, never washed or brushed, was a mouldering off-white, like an ancient tuft of sheep's wool caught on a barbed-wire fence. The sour cast of his features was unrelenting. Listless, lost in constant recollection, he was isolated by a bitterness that pervaded his every word and gesture.

Aware he was under scrutiny, Eamon turned sharply. 'What?' he grunted.

'You know what'll happen if that fellow hides out here. We'll get jail, Eamon, nothing surer.'

'He won't come,' Eamon muttered, his face creased with anxiety. 'But if he does, I won't let him down. I owe him.'

'He's a psycho — he's been out of control for years, and you know it,' Robby said.

Eamon dismissed the suggestion with a wave of the poker. 'Don't let anyone see you with the rifle,' he said. 'We don't want to give them shaggin' guards any excuses to be hanging around the place. And, hey, I set another of those badger-traps up at that ditch. See if I caught anything.'

'I told you not to be setting those things. What if the cattle stray into it?'

'It's my land. I'll set what I want on it.'

Robby got one hand free from holding Rusty just long enough to slam the door behind him. Inside, the poker fell or was thrown. It rang out like a bell.

ᏣᏵ

In the end, the stone circle at Cloghercree hadn't been so difficult to locate. On the long drive from the Dun Laoghaire ferry-port, Bubble's carefully compiled map had proven surprisingly accurate — surprisingly because Mayfly Blenthyne's father was, in her eyes, the most careless of men.

The pink and yellow dormobile struggled up a steep, swerving incline between the overhanging hedges on the narrow road. Bubble's demented brush of greying dreadlocks whirled in the breeze from the open window. He urged the machine upwards as if his mad yelps of encouragement made a difference.

'Come on, Nirvana, nearly there, man,' he shouted into the rushing air that carried his words back along the road with the cloud of dusty fumes. 'I do believe, I do believe we're almost there!' For all his years as a musician in America and his later wanderings from country to country, Bubble had never quite lost the clipped accent of his English public-school days.

The dormobile, a converted delivery van, swept out of the dark green shadows; and there, as Bubble had predicted, was the object of their foolish quest. Distant but clearly visible, the standing stones formed a grey, unimpressive crown on the crest of a low hill.

Mayfly turned to her sleeping mother and fixed the multicoloured woollen Rasta hat which covered the delicate pate of her hairless head and the stark, bleached white of the bandage.

'About time,' she muttered. 'You said three hours. We've been on the road for five.'

Bubble's grip on the steering wheel tightened, but his smile remained fixed and his gaze still tried to make something wondrous of the crooked, stony stumps.

'You won't do it for me,' he said, 'but for Andy's sake, make an effort, will you?'

'To do what? To believe in a heap of dumb stones? They won't undo what you did to Andy.'

The optimistic, starry sparkle in his eyes clouded over. 'That's unfair,' he said, his shoulders slumping wearily.

'Right. Living in a scrap-heap was good for her, then. No

place to call home, always on the road, smoking hash ....'

'Everything we did, we did together,' Bubble said, slowing the dormobile down, touching the indicator.

'And this journey hasn't helped ....'

Mayfly fell silent. On the right-hand side of the road ahead, a cemetery came into view. Slabs of polished stone reflecting pale replicas of sunlight; frostlike beds of white pebbles; an old man on a stick disappearing along the path between tall, spiralling evergreens. They passed into a laneway barely wide enough for the dormobile.

'No one's going to stop you making your own way,' Bubble told her, as the thin branches of hedgerow whipped and slapped against the dormobile. 'When the time comes. I mean, if .... You know what I mean.'

'Yeah, right,' Mayfly said. 'Like I've got choices. Like you left me any choices.'

The laneway widened and Bubble steered Nirvana onto a flat verge of grass. Nirvana — heaven, the ultimate state of well-being, fulfilment, happiness. Nirvana, reeking of burnt motor oil and hot as the pit of hell.

Andy stirred from her sleep. The smile, that smile of exasperating calmness, came even before her eyes opened.

'We made it, then.' Andy's voice had changed, over these past two years, from a high-pitched Texas twang to a lazy drawl, the voice of a stranger. She peered out at the rolling fields, the shambling outcrop of stones scrawled against the cloudless June sky. The remnant of some dream momentarily creased the pallid skin of her forehead. Then the disturbance passed, or she let it pass.

'Good old Nirvana,' Andy said. 'Know something, guys? This old machine's gonna keep on going forever.'

chapter 2

The four-barred gate into the Stone Field was tied fast with a length of white electrical cord. The five wide acres, quite flat except for the stone-capped hillock away to the left, were no longer used by Eamon. A neighbouring farmer, Mick Johnston, had leased the field for the past two years. He let the grass grow long and cut it for silage to feed the cattle on his own, much larger farm.

Each New Year's Eve, Mick came and sat at the kitchen table with Eamon. There, they drank whiskey from the good Waterford glasses and haggled good-humouredly over the price of the next year's lease. Each time, Eamon's protests grew weaker when Mick got around to asking if he'd sell the field outright. They never spoke about it, but Robby was sure his great-uncle would soon give in, and he knew why. Eamon believed in the curse of the Stone Field.

The Wades had first come to Cloghercree in the early 1880s, when Thaddeus, Robby's great-great-grandfather, bought what was then a two-hundred-acre farm. Unlike his new neighbours, Thaddeus wasn't superstitious. He announced that the stone circle would have to go, and laughed off their warning protests. His own three sons weren't old enough or strong enough to help, and his daughter was too sickly. So he looked for volunteers, promising to pay them well. All he got in answer was a fearfully repeated 'You'll have no luck for it'.

Returning from his first day digging around the tallest of the stones, he found his wife screaming blame at him for the dead daughter in her arms. Since then, every

generation of Wades had been blighted by some tragedy
— right down to Robby's father, whose parents before
him had died in a car accident in 1966. There had been
lesser tragedies, too — three successive potato harvests
destroyed, in the 1970s, while the neighbours' crops survived; a TB outbreak in the herd back in the 80s. To Robby,
the curse was merely a pathetic excuse for the Wades'
failures.

Stroking the dog's lumpy, trembling spine, Robby
placed Rusty on the grass by the gate. There had never
been a time when Rusty had not been a part of his life.

'Don't go running off on me now, boy,' he said, but the
dog looked at Robby as if he knew, as if he wanted it to end.

Through the bars of the gate Robby saw, at the far end
of the field, the white-walled cottage beyond the grove
where Rusty would lie forever. A few years before, he
would have seen a well-worn path winding from the
cottage, up past the stones, to this gate — a gate that was
never closed, back then. Mick Johnston's regular cutting
of the grass had left hardly a trace of that path, and the
cottage where Robby had grown up lay deserted.

Beyond the cottage, the narrow back road was a grey
ribbon with a green stripe decorating its centre. Robby's
eye moved instinctively along it, hoping not to find any
cars or vans parked there. Eamon didn't welcome visitors
to the stones.

The flash of yellow and pink, just visible through the
full summery growth of hedgerow, startled him. An ice-
cream van, perhaps, its owner having a bite of lunch or a
quiet escape from the demands of excited children?
Robby half-expected to hear the tinny chimes ring out a
nursery-rhyme tune, a little off-key like a child's first
singing efforts.

'I'll be back in a minute, Rusty,' he said, and went
along by the ditch.

He found the shovel twenty yards away, its timber weathered to white, the rusted metal caked with dried clay. Nearby, he came across the badger-trap, camouflaged neatly among the folds of briar in the ditch. Along its three-foot span, filed metal teeth awaited the next of its many victims. Eamon had made the trap years ago and prided himself on his ingenuity. All his traps, those for badgers and foxes and rats, had spring-locks only he could release.

Robby tore a branch from the heavier growth above and stripped it to a stick. Nothing stirred, not a leaf nor a bird's wing, and there was not a sound from the distant back road. He lowered the stick between the jaws of the trap.

Under the mid-afternoon sun, Robby shivered. Around him, the world seemed dizzily vast, with its endless tapestry of fields and the enormity and sheer blueness of the sky. But how easily that sight, that sense of astonishment, could be blasted away into eternal darkness! One bullet was all it had taken for Sean Wade. One bullet was all it had taken for the part-time soldier he and the others had ambushed. One bullet was all it would take for Rusty.

He moved the stick so that it barely grazed the point of a single jagged tooth in the trap. Instantly, the stick was sliced in two with a force that shuddered through Robby's hand and along his forearm.

He walked back to the gate and, his hand still tingling icily, began to fumble with the knotted cord. At a bite-shaped gap in the hedge down by the back road, a woman in a long white dress appeared — a ghostlike figure but for the multicoloured hat she wore. The quick calculation in Robby's mind — the yellow and pink van, the oddly dressed woman — offered only one possible conclusion. New Age types — for Eamon, the most despised of all visitors to Cloghercree. 'Knackers, English spongers' — English because, in Eamon's reasoning, everything English was bad and everything bad was English.

Whenever Robby was forced to listen to his great-uncle's rantings on the subject, he envied the freedom and easy-going lives of the few hippies and backpackers who came to Cloghercree. Even Tommy the Tramp, who often called to the farm on his wanderings and slept in the old Ford Cortina out in the garage, provoked this secret longing in him. Unwashed, penniless, rarely sober, Tommy at least was free. His habit of calling Robby by Sean's name was an irritating reminder of their likeness, but his confusion was genuine; Tommy would never knowingly hurt anyone. Unlike Eamon and Robby — tearing each other's heart out like drowning cats in a bag.

Now that Robby was about to lose the only living creature he cared for, that unspoken envy ran deeper than ever before.

⟶⟵

When Bubble had announced his plan to bring them to Ireland, Mayfly had been none too impressed. And that was even before he'd mentioned his crazy theory about the stones. She worried about how Andy would cope with the journey. And why Ireland?

'It's a wonderful place, man,' Bubble had said. 'Went there when I was a boy. Good people, you know? They take the time to talk to each other and —'

'And kill each other,' was Mayfly's withering reply.

'Things are different there now, Fly,' he'd insisted. 'Always were, where we're going. Down south.'

Mayfly advanced along the grassy trapeze dividing the pebbled tracks, glad of the cool breeze that greeted her at the bend in the lane. At least in Ireland she wouldn't have to suffer the summer swelter of last year in Morocco. In Marrakesh, the heat had been a thick substance to be swum in rather than walked through. The summer before, it had been Eastern Europe — the Czech Republic, Hungary; not quite as hot, but often as unpleasant, with its dusty airlessness, its sense of being too far from the cooling sea.

As far back as Mayfly's memory stretched, there had been these summer trips. Bubble and Andy cobbled together the money through long, damp English winters. So many places, all of them exotic for a while — until things went wrong, which they invariably did.

Bubble and Andy would arrive, their eyes childlike with wonder, their hearts full of hope that, at last, they'd found the perfect place. Then Bubble would get himself arrested for possession of cannabis and they'd be thrown out of the country. Or they'd be harassed by the police or the locals, simply for daring to be different, and they'd leave of their own accord, bemused as ever by people's intolerance.

Some life. Going nowhere the long way round was how Mayfly saw it. For herself, she wanted a life that served some useful purpose. Imagining what that purpose might be helped to keep her mind from the impending catastrophe of her mother's death; it was another barricade to add to her inner defences, another mind-game among many. But what chance did she have, in the run-down schools she was condemned to as they moved from one encampment or commune to the next? As for her hopes of going to university — that would cost more money than they'd ever see.

Unlike Bubble, Mayfly would never have the opportunity to spit the silver spoon from her mouth. Her grandfather, Sir Gordon Blenthyne, might be one of the richest men in England, but she'd never met him and knew virtually nothing about him. Bubble rarely spoke of his father, and when he did, it was in the vaguest and most disdainful of terms — 'capitalist scum', 'one of the rotten rich'.

Mayfly had long ago outgrown the fantasy that Sir Gordon would someday hail Bubble as his prodigal son and change her life for the better, sending her to the best schools, the most prestigious universities. The stark reality was that, as Andy slept in the dormobile and Mayfly wandered along the leafy lane, Bubble had gone in search of a supply of hash, with a fistful of grubby fivers.

'It helps to ease her pain, you know that,' he'd asserted as he got ready to walk the mile and a half into town. 'To ease her mind, man.'

'Yeah, right,' Mayfly had answered. 'So why are you smoking more hash than she is?'

'My pain —' he began.

'I'm hurting too, Bubble, but I'm not smoking myself stupid like you are.'

The lane took another of its lazy curves, and up ahead an abandoned cottage came into view. Abstract flashes of sunlight reflected from broken window-panes; white paint was blistered and cracked on the walls; a ragged mesh of briars and tall weeds crept along the small front garden, pointing bent, skeletal fingers through windows and half-open door. Mayfly made her way along the overgrown privet hedge at the side of the cottage. Behind, a dense thicket of oak trees formed a grove, and she passed through until she found its sunlit core.

Here, the silence was deeper and more easeful. The sun's warmth, too, was comforting, and it drew a stretch and yawn of mellow tiredness from Mayfly. She lay down on the grass, spreading out the green summer dress that made a chameleon of her in that verdant place. Sweeping back the wisps of gold-red hair from about her face, she closed her eyes, turning the blue sky into a bright red glow.

All the while, she fought against the guilt brewing up in her — guilt for allowing herself this pleasure, this brief escape from her mother. The game she played was an old one: Rainbow Shades. Think of a colour; think of every shade of that colour you can remember. Take blue. Navy, royal, sky, azure, indigo, ultramarine ....

ಣ

Robby passed by the stone circle, faltering under his awkward load. Rifle, shovel, Rusty. The dog's eyes were sad and trusting and very tired. The vivid sleekness of the fine red hair was gone; pink flesh showed through in patches, freckled like diseased autumn leaves. Fifteen years wasn't a bad span for a setter. But for the poison, he might have had a few more; a slower, less adventurous life, perhaps, but a comfortable one, with Robby to take care of him. That wasn't to be, and Robby had stopped thinking about the unfairness of it.

The shovel and the rifle clanged together, as if to stir him, and his pace quickened.

ಣ

In the heart of the grove, Mayfly was woken abruptly by the sound. The swish of grass in the field behind grew louder by the second.

On all fours, she launched herself towards the nearest of the thick-trunked oaks. Finding cover, she heard a young man's voice.

'We'll rest here, Rusty.'

A dog barked, very weakly, and Mayfly dared to peer out from her hiding-place.

'We can go hunting ... afterwards.'

He was tall, very tall, and wore black combats and a long-sleeved, V-necked black T-shirt. His short black hair was swept untidily forward. The long, narrow sideburns seemed oddly out of place on the young face. His gaze never left the dog as he backed out of Mayfly's view.

'Over there, Rusty, look over there ... at the trees ... the birds,' Robby pleaded; but the dog stared at him, dared him.

He picked up the rifle, checked the breach again and snapped off the safety catch. He steeled himself and began to advance on his target. In his mind, the part-time soldier's van was pulling into that Fermanagh farmyard, and he was Sean Wade, looking to the other members of the ambush gang for the signal to shoot. Looking to Eamon, and to Razor McCabe, and to Liam O'Neill.

The trigger's resistance weakened. Salty sweat bothered the corners of his eyes. A shudder passed through him, and with it went all pity. He wanted to kill Rusty, to punish him for his weakness, for his stupid trust, for being a sheep-killer.

'You don't deserve to live,' he whispered.

From his left side came a whirring blur of green and gold. Something hard whipped into his elbow and the rifle spun upwards, loosing a shot into the trees as the girl threw herself to her knees at Rusty's side. A flock of birds erupted from above in a panic of leaves and wings.

# chapter 3

'Murderer!' Mayfly cried. 'Turn that gun away from me!'

She held the dog close to her and shot a hostile glance at Robby. She was bathed in the light of the clearing. He stood, pale in the shade of the trees, the rifle dragging his arms down. By Mayfly's side, the dog lurched and a yellow bile emerged from its mouth.

'She's been poisoned, hasn't she?' she asked angrily. 'Have you had her seen to? Or do you prefer acting the —'

'*Him.* The vet said he was finished,' Robby said. 'You're one of those hippies, aren't you?'

'So?' she said. 'You got a problem with that?'

Robby raised his rifle and held it firmly crosswise in both hands.

'You're trespassing,' he told her, nodding towards the road and the square of timber staked to the ditch. 'Can you not read, or what?'

Mayfly hadn't noticed the sign, large as it was, but that was too absurd to admit. The dog pressed closer and she comforted it with her touch. But her touch wouldn't be enough. The familiar sense of powerlessness intensified her anger. If she'd inherited anything from Andy and Bubble, it was impetuousness. But saving the dog from being shot was one thing. Ending its obvious suffering was another.

'You know what you look like? Like one of those dumb dolls they give little boys. Action Man. Bet you got dozens of them in your playroom.'

The beginnings of a blush appeared on his high cheek-bones. Mayfly raised herself to her knees, keeping her stare fixed so as to deepen his discomfort.

'I'm on my way, Action Man. And I'm taking *him* with me.'

Swaying as she lifted the dog, she heard the sliding bolt on Robby's gun.

'Put him down,' Robby warned. 'He's dying. He's in pain — has to be put out of his misery.'

Mayfly nudged a small picket gate open and stepped into the back garden of the dilapidated cottage. Robby hadn't yet moved.

'What's his name? What did you call him before you ...?'

'He's dying,' Robby repeated in a dull monotone. 'He doesn't need a name where he's going.'

'You've been watching too many videos, Action Man,' Mayfly said, and remembered. 'Rusty. It was Rusty, wasn't it?'

Among the snaking whorls of briar in the cottage garden, a few small flowers had survived, adding a dash of forlorn colour to the chaos. Mayfly's green dress snagged and tore as she reached the gable end of the cottage.

'You're nothing but a bunch of wasters, the lot of you,' he shouted after her. 'If I see any of you knackers around here again, I'll shoot. Don't think I wouldn't.'

Just as she turned the corner of the cottage, another shot ricocheted through the trees high above. She stumbled against the cottage wall. Flakes of peeling whitewash clung to her hair like a dry snow. She pushed breathlessly on, through the thorny undergrowth, to the front gate.

Out on the back road at last, the dog whimpering in her arms, she found herself standing below the 'No Trespassing' sign. The green-painted lettering was crudely out of line, and the final 'N' and 'G' were squashed together to make them fit. The work of a simple, disordered mind, its message all the more sinister for that. So much for Bubble's stone fantasy, with natives like these guarding their precious fields.

Some part of her hoped the young gunman would follow and wrench the dog from her. A brief struggle, even a few painful blows, would ease whatever pangs of conscience she might suffer later. But he didn't come, and she hadn't really expected him to.

It wasn't as though Mayfly had any great love for dogs. Once, she had taken the usual childhood pleasure in playing with puppies. But every encampment they'd ever lived in had been littered with dogs, too many of them mangy with neglect. Andy and Bubble had no great desire to keep dogs either — which was just as well, considering they had such difficulty taking care of themselves. There was little enough room in the dormobile as it was, and the presence of a dying dog was hardly desirable now.

She looked back at the cottage, its front door leaning invitingly inwards. It seemed as good a shelter as any, and it was the last place Action Man would expect her to bring the dog.

Through the laurel hedge at the roadside wall, she watched Robby make his way back past the stone circle. When he'd gone through the gate at the other end of the field and passed out of sight, Mayfly moved as quickly as Rusty's bulk allowed. The path, half-cleared by her trampling escape, was mercifully short, so she had enough strength left to elbow the door aside. The frail timber slipped a little further on its hinges but held fast.

Andy often spoke about the spirits she perceived in places they visited. She'd talk about the 'seriously evil vibes' radiating from some old building. Towns, whole countries — usually ones they were about to be kicked out of — received a verdict of 'Bad karma, time to go'. People, too: 'Don't like the aura round that guy,' she'd say. There were good vibes, karma and auras, too, though more rarely of late.

As Mayfly stood among the shards of broken glass in the dusty kitchen, what she experienced was something in between those poles of good and evil. An atmosphere of spent anger, a loneliness beyond tears. The cobwebs, wide and all-encompassing, were like a veil between the living and the dead.

Mayfly was only half-afraid to be there. Less afraid than she was in Nirvana.

∽

The stone floor drew sparks from the trap's clenched metal bow.

'It was already sprung,' Robby said. 'I'm throwing it in the cellar along with all your other contraptions.'

Eamon glanced at the trap and turned his attention back to the TV. 'Put it where you like, Robby. I'll set it again if I need to,' he answered offhandedly. 'Did you shoot the dog?'

'Yeah, I shot him. Didn't you hear?' Robby shouted above the noise from the portable black-and-white TV. The picture was so snowy that most of the time you had to guess what was happening. Since Eamon only ever bothered to watch the news, this was easy enough to do.

'Did you not hit him the first time?'

'I just wanted to make sure. That's what you're supposed to do, isn't it?'

In the Fermanagh ambush — the Wades' one and only taste of active service — the first shot smashed the UDR man's left collarbone but wasn't fatal. Sean Wade died instantly in the return of fire. One shot to the heart. Eamon, crouched on the back slope of a galvanised roof, lost his balance as he dodged a second shot from the part-time soldier. He fell ten feet, his left leg twisted under him, the femur snapping on impact, the kneecap driven round to the back. The next round, McCabe's, fired from four or five feet away, hit the base of Alan Wilson's skull.

From there, it travelled down his spine, severing all the
nerve connections and sending him into the paralysed
coma from which he never woke — the paralysed coma
that had become Robby's recurring nightmare.

They didn't find Alan Wilson until early the next
morning. By then, Eamon was at the local hospital, taken
there by some Republican friends who claimed to have
witnessed his fall from the barn roof at Cloghercree. No
one was ever charged with the murder, though Razor
McCabe and Liam O'Neill, the fourth gunman, had been
jailed for IRA membership soon after.

'You shouldn't be wasting bullets, Robby. They're not
easy to get.'

'You'll hardly be needing them any more.'

'Maybe not.' Eamon eyed him sharply. 'But you never
know.'

'I'm doing up a fry,' Robby said, avoiding another bitter exchange. 'Do you want some?'

Eamon nodded and, leaning forward on his battered
old armchair, gazed at the TV screen apprehensively. He'd
switched on the TV a good ten minutes before the news
was due to start.

Robby considered the tense, drawn face. How could he
ever have attributed greatness to this man? Or listened in
such tearful rapture to his songs? 'The Men Behind the
Wire', 'The Fields of Athenry', 'The Dying Rebel' ....

My only son was shot in Dublin,
Fighting for his country bold.
He died for Ireland and Ireland only,
The harp and shamrock, green, white and gold ....

'For Ireland and Ireland only' — Sean Wade's epitaph,
the letters etched and painted black on the grey, polished
base of a tall Celtic cross in Cloghercree cemetery.

As a child, Robby had sung those lines, alone in the
cottage bedroom, and the tears he wanted no one else to

see had flowed freely. It had been easy, then, to swear that he too would die willingly for that cause. Once, he'd dared to say so to his mother. His reward had been a slap across the face, and then a smothering, apologetic hug. 'Ireland only,' she'd cried. 'And what about the rest of us?'

In spite of his confusion, Robby had held to his belief. Back then, he had been too young to notice the locals whispering about the recklessness of a thirty-eight-year-old Eamon dragging his nineteen-year-old nephew along with him to Fermanagh; too young, too, to notice the dwindling crowds at the annual Republican gathering by Sean Wade's grave. At last year's ceremony, there had been three people present; three and a half if you counted Robby standing in the next field, listening to those ghostly voices in prayer.

While his schoolmates had rarely mentioned his father, there had been the occasional bully who'd taunted him for being 'the gunman's orphan'. He'd learned, however, to see off his tormentors with a brutal ferocity that surprised even himself. It was a quality that gained him no favour, only a grudging respect and a mistrust that left him friendless.

'Will you give over that bloody racket,' Eamon bawled.

Robby didn't protest. The noise of banging pots and cupboard doors was deliberate. He was trying to drown out the memory of that final argument between Liam O'Neill and Eamon, two years before. Eamon had despised O'Neill since he'd left the IRA, and the thought of this traitor to the cause marrying Sean's sweetheart had been too much for him to take.

'We were defending the Nationalist people of Northern Ireland.'

'Yeah, it started out like that, Eamon, but it got so it wasn't about people any more. It was about territory and driving the Protestants out. It was about revenge.'

'They deserved everything they got. Them and the bloody

Brits, propping up a rotten, corrupt state for fifty years.'

'It's changed, Eamon. Or changing.'

'Changing, my arse. Would you be a Catholic in Portadown, O'Neill? Would you run the gauntlet of those Loyalist mobs, night, noon and morning?'

'So we start shooting them? We start the whole tit-for-tat thing all over again?'

'Don't be making excuses for yourself, O'Neill. You took the easy way out. You walked away from your comrades.'

'Yeah, I took the easy way out. And so did the ones who kept the killing going. The hard way is to put down the gun and start talking, even when you're dealing with men who've walked all over you. The hard way is to believe they can change, if you can. Can't you see that?'

'Nothing will ever change in the North. Not until Ireland is given back to the Irish. Not until there's a united Ireland. That's what Sean died for.'

Eamon's textbook answer — coming, as it did, on the night Robby was losing his mother — didn't seem like a good reason to have lost a father as well.

Only Grace's tears kept O'Neill and Eamon from trading blows. When she spoke, the rawness of her pain silenced both of them.

'Sean was just a boy who never, never, never had the chance to grow up!'

The tears Robby had kept hidden below the bedclothes for years welled up, and when his mother tried to touch him he pushed her away. The voice, breaking between a high-pitched wail and a deep roar, was not his own.

'I hate him! I hate the whole bloody lot of you! I wish I'd never been born!'

From the TV, a dramatic burst of music signalled the news programme and blasted away the memory from Robby's mind. Eamon went down on one knee, reaching across to turn the sound up even higher.

The announcer's tone was gravely urgent.

'Gardaí are still searching for the former Republican prisoner, Michael "Razor" McCabe .... The kidnap victim, businessman Stephen Buckley, is recovering at the Mater Hospital ... severe mutilation .... Garda Thomas Spillane, injured during the rescue of Mr Buckley, is in intensive care ... gunshot wounds .... The public are advised not to approach ... is armed ... likely, garda sources say, to be moving towards the Midlands .... Because of McCabe's rift with the Republican movement, few "safe houses" are thought to be available to him.'

Robby turned from the cooker, where the sausages and rashers had begun to sizzle. He didn't know when Eamon had last sheltered any of his former comrades. It hadn't happened in the two years Robby had lived there, but that very fact might make it a safer place for someone on the run. McCabe was a maverick, shunned by the IRA because he'd siphoned off some of the takings from several bank robberies he'd carried out with them; but he was still a hero to Eamon.

The announcer had moved on to reports of trouble in the Middle East, but Eamon's pretended interest didn't fool Robby.

'He's coming here, isn't he?'

'What? Yasser Arafat? Imagine that little lad walking up the Cloghercree Road with the tea-towel on his head!'

'Razor McCabe. Your *friend*. Mr Mutilator.'

Eamon poked viciously at the fire, sending red sparks onto the square of linoleum by the hearth, making no attempt to stamp them out.

'They make up all that stuff,' he said.

Robby stared at his great-uncle in disbelief, but resisted the temptation to get sidetracked.

'Is he coming here?' he repeated evenly. 'Because if he is ....'

'Whatever else he is,' Eamon said, pointing the reddened

poker at Robby, 'he's not an eejit. The guards'll be all over us until they find him. He'll know that.'

The smell of burning meat sent Robby spinning around to grab the frying-pan's handle. Too hot, it slipped from his grasp to the floor. Streaks of hot grease ran down his combats and stung through to his flesh. He looked at the mess on the floor. If he didn't clean it up, no one ever would.

Why not walk out that door, leave it all behind — his crippled great-uncle, this mess, the bigger mess in his head? Why not walk away from everything, go on the road like Tommy the Tramp or those New Agers, like that girl? What was there to stay for? Some vague promise that Eamon would let him run the farm properly when he was 'old enough'? Robby had taken that to mean when he was eighteen; but what would be left of the farm by then? If Eamon sold the Stone Field, they'd be left with ninety acres. And who was to say it would stop there? People were calling all the time to ask if he'd any house sites for sale — the place was ideal for them, being so near the fast-expanding town ....

'What did you mean, anyway?' Eamon demanded. '"Because if he is ...." If he is, what? What'll you do?'

'Nothing.'

'You don't have to stay, you know. You can always go back to your mother. And your *stepfather*. *Step* is right. Stepping all over your father's grave.'

chapter 4

The dormobile swayed like a moored boat as Mayfly
stepped through, cautiously so as not to disturb her
mother. The temporary blindness of coming inside from
the bright day was no hindrance. Every cramped square
inch of the place was familiar to her. On her left, the wood
stove whose fumes pervaded everything; the tiny sink
without taps; the gas cooker. Along the right-hand side,
the bed where Andy lay sleeping, which when raised up
became a table; the sitting-area, consisting of three bean-
bags and a pile of cushions collected on their travels; the
big black plastic bags which contained everything from
clothes to food to books and tapes, to keep them from
getting damp. On the walls, dead rock stars gazed down
from their yellowing age — Jimi Hendrix, Janis Joplin,
Jim Morrison, Tim Buckley — and Bubble's guitar hung
crossways over the door like a shotgun in an old Western
movie.

At the far end, another door, so small Mayfly had to
stoop to pass through, led to her own private compartment.
Inside, her eyes readjusted themselves to the sun streaming in through the skylight. A delicately woven Indian
rug covered the small window into the dormobile's cab.

Mayfly sat on the fold-up bed which took up half the
minuscule space. A shelf, clamped to the wall and dou-
bling as a kind of table, was all she had in the way of
furniture. Beneath this she kept her possessions, in one of
four rubbish bags which couldn't be squeezed into the
main cabin. The rest were filled with her parents' things,
and it was one of these she drew towards her.

The knotted plastic crinkled noisily. Mayfly hesitated and listened for some sound from the main cabin. There was none, except the repeated sigh of Andy's low breathing. She teased open the knot and began to take out the books, one by one. Musty old paperbacks, their kaleidoscopic pop-art covers faded, fell apart at the touch of her hand.

The absence of new books was proof that her parents' minds had gone lazy a long time ago. The life they led, or had led until Andy's illness, confirmed that. Their days of mystic adventure and environmental activism were long past. All they lived for was summer — and the road.

Three or four books remained in the bottom of the bag. A quick glance confirmed that the one Mayfly was looking for lay elsewhere. She — and Rusty, lying under the torn linen sheet she'd found at the cottage — would have to wait until Andy woke to search for a cure.

Nature's Magical Gift was a book on herbalism — one of the few passions her parents had once indulged in that Mayfly thought in any way worthwhile.

Andy didn't cook any more, but all the strictly vegetarian recipes that Mayfly had learned from her mother required herbs. The cuts and sores of Mayfly's childhood, too, had invariably been healed with herbal poultices.

Like all the other alternative medicines, however, the herbs had failed Andy. A tumour as advanced as hers was more than a poison. It was the body attacking itself.

A poison, though, could be expelled, and the herbs might just do that. If it wasn't too late. That was the other thing: taking action quickly enough, not being stupid or careless. Yes, the herbs might work for Rusty, at least. They might save him when they couldn't save Andy — who, in the end, had come to rely on only one herb: cannabis. And cannabis cured nothing, offered only a temporary escape.

Mayfly refilled the plastic sack and stared dismally at the miniature picture gallery that decorated the wall behind her bed. Photographs of friends met and lost as she had moved on from one town, one school, to the next. And photographs of Andy and Bubble in their hippie heyday: Bubble performing at music festivals with a variety of anonymous bands; the pair of them, smiling or angry or plain strung-out, at anti-nuclear protest meetings; Andy, in suitably hazy repose among the long grasses of the Californian communal farm where they'd met.

'Mayfly?'

Mayfly opened the door into the cabin, slowly, so that the light wouldn't burst through but ease inwards like a friend. Andy, floating upwards into waking, was more frail than ever. Her eyelids flickered in trembling harmony with her unsteady hands on the bedcovers.

'You had a good sleep,' Mayfly said, sitting on the edge of the bed.

'I sure did.' Andy's shaven and bandaged head swayed on the pillow. 'I think I woke earlier. There was a loud bang — a dog barking .... Guess I was dreaming ....'

'What would you like to eat this evening?' Mayfly said hastily, for how could she be so cruel as to ask about cures for a poisoned dog from someone who could find none for herself? 'Will I do a curry?'

Andy smiled and raised herself on one elbow, testing her balance. 'We have to talk, Mayfly,' she said. 'Talk it all through. I've been putting this off too long.'

'Remember the book you had about herbs? Do you know which bag it's in?'

'Fly, we can't bury this away ....'

'Don't say that word. Please.'

'Sorry. Bad choice of phrase, but —'

'The book ... the herbs ....' Mayfly pleaded.

'I can just about remember where my head is.' Andy

chuckled and touched the bandage. 'Up here somewhere, right?'

'Why do you have to *joke* about it, Andy?' Mayfly cried.

She stood up, making herself busy around the cabin. She picked up her mother's white dress from the floor and folded it. She opened the curtains and tied them back. Glad to see the dust and dirt, she set to work with the brush and pan. All the while, she was aware of Andy, who'd sunk back on the pillow and was watching her every move. The unwelcome attention made clumsy claws of her busy hands.

'Fly?'

'What about the book?' Mayfly asked, desperate to distract her mother.

'Tell me what you need to know. See if I can make sense of what's left in here.'

'Stop talking like that!' Mayfly flung the brush onto the floor. 'Sorry, it fell, it just fell ....' She scrambled across the grimy floor to retrieve the brush.

'Fly, talk to me.'

And then, because it was impossible to speak of what really mattered, she told Andy about the dog. She didn't mention Action Man and his gun.

'Poison? Depends on the type, of course, but .... OK, poison hits the system — liver, kidneys. So you'll need a purgative ... a diuretic, too. Dandelion, nettle. Yeah, and maybe bamboo shoots for detoxification. And ginger, basil, to clean out the system ....'

'All of them? Together? You mean, like, boil them up together or something?'

Andy nodded and leaned forward to rest her head on her knees.

'Are you all right?' Mayfly asked. 'I shouldn't have brought this up.'

'Sure, no problem. Weird what you can dredge up when you push it, Fly. Yeah, teaspoon of each to half a litre of water.'

Outside the dormobile, the stillness was disturbed by a loud screech of anxious birdsong, followed by the rhythm of approaching footsteps. Bubble, no doubt, back with his supplies. Andy took up her Rasta hat from beside the pillow and fixed it over the bandage. Her drawn features assumed that annoying lovestruck look that always greeted Bubble's return from his ramblings.

'Never was much of an expert on animals, though,' she said. 'Never understood that. I mean, OK, I don't eat them! But I never, you know, connected with cats and dogs and all.'

'You can't love everything.'

'Sure you can. You just gotta make the effort. Every creature deserves affection, right?' Andy stirred herself and brightened again. 'Anyway, if that mix don't kill the dog, it'll sure as hell make its hair grow!'

She reached for Mayfly's hand and pressed it to her cheek.

'We're in this together, Fly, all three of us,' she said. 'This isn't anyone's fault. It doesn't have to be anyone's fault.'

Mayfly turned her face away. Rainbow Shades. Black: pitch, coal, ebony .... She saw her father's faint outline through the grimy glass as he sauntered along the grass-tufted centre of the lane. She closed her eyes. Jet, ink, charcoal ....

The game ended abruptly when she looked out again.

The ragged figure framed in the dusty window wasn't Bubble.

chapter 5

'That's right, he's as thick as you lot are.' Eamon stared down Detective Sergeant Pat Healy, gripping the poker for strength. 'He's below in the cellar, waiting to give himself up.'

From the kitchen door, a uniformed guard advanced threateningly. He pushed Robby aside, but the heavy-set detective intervened before he reached Eamon. Healy spoke quietly, the tolerant grin never leaving his face.

'Wait outside, John, while I have a chat with the saviour of Ireland here, OK?' he ordered.

When his companion had retreated, he sat down at the kitchen table and removed the flat cap that left an encircling crease on his bald scalp.

'Have you tea on, Robby?'

Uneasy as ever in Healy's presence, Robby nodded but didn't speak. Eamon's and Sean's reputations apart, there was another reason for this unease.

Pat Healy coached at the local hurling club. Three years before, Robby had failed to turn up for an Under-14s county final. Robby didn't imagine his absence had made the difference, but the team had lost. He'd never been able to tell Healy why he hadn't been there — a fight with one of his team-mates earlier in the day, the others taking sides against him. Soon after that, he'd given up hurling altogether. Sometimes he wondered if he'd just been looking for a reason to stop playing. He loved hurling, but he was constantly being compared to his father, and he hated it because he knew he'd never be as good as Sean Wade.

Healy sipped the tea Robby poured for him. 'Cripes,

that's a bit on the strong side,' he said. 'Any chance of a drop of milk?'

Robby went to the fridge that was dotted with dirty fingerprints and pawmarks. Inside, on the shelf below the milk, lay a bag of bones he'd got for Rusty only two days before.

'There was shots heard up here, Eamon,' Healy said bluntly. 'What do you make of that?'

'Don't have a gun,' Eamon replied. 'You wouldn't give me a licence, remember?'

'Well, sure, John can have a poke around outside. Never know what he'd come up with.'

The milk came out in a sputtering, nervous stream as Robby poured. Healy looked about the grotty kitchen.

'Where's Rusty?' he asked, and drank another draught of the tepid tea.

'Out in the fields, I suppose,' Robby said.

Through the kitchen window, he watched the young guard enter the barn. He hoped Healy hadn't noticed his dismay.

'God, this is great,' Eamon interjected. 'The forces of law and order looking for missing dogs to go running after. You haven't much to be doing, have you?'

'We've plenty of dogs to chase after, Wade. Razor McCabe, for one. He cut off that man's ear, did you know that? There's a heroic act for you, now. Cutting a man's ear off.'

'A pity he didn't cut yours off, Healy. And your big lump of a nose along with it.'

For a big man, Healy moved quickly. Just as the chair hit the floor behind the rugged policeman, Eamon found himself pinned against the wall. Sickened by Healy's revelation, Robby didn't feel much like defending his great-uncle. Outside, the guard appeared at the barn door, empty-handed, and went to search the outhouses.

Out of sheer instinct, Robby moved towards the struggling pair. Glancing over his shoulder, Healy warned, 'Stay out of it, Robby.' Then, turning his attention to Eamon again, he went on, 'The gloves are off, Wade. Anyone gets in the way of us catching that scumbag, we'll trample all over them.'

Eamon ignored Healy's fierce gaze and punished Robby with an accusing look.

Healy let him go and turned to Robby. 'Don't get mixed up in this, son,' he said. 'Go back to your mother and O'Neill. He's a sensible man, not like the brave Eamon here.'

Ë

When Healy had left, they sat back down at the table. The grease from the rashers on their plates had hardened to waxy puddles. Eamon stared at the food with contempt.

'He's making up that stuff about McCabe cutting off the fellow's ear, is he?' Robby asked, disgusted.

'I'll tell you one thing, Robby boy. You could depend on McCabe. He wouldn't have let Healy push me around, like you did.'

The sour heat of Eamon's breath deepened Robby's disgust. He pushed his chair back and stood above his great-uncle.

'You know something?' he said. 'When I look at you and that ... that animal McCabe on the telly, and that other two-faced jerk O'Neill, you know what I think? I think my father was the lucky one. At least he didn't end up like you lot.'

Eamon launched himself from his chair, stumbling awkwardly forward without his stick.

'McCabe saved me that day in Fermanagh. O'Neill wanted to drive away and leave me there, but McCabe came back for me. That's a *man*, Robby, that's a bloody hero of a man. And what was his reward? Drummed out of the IRA on O'Neill's say-so. Is it any wonder he —'

'He went crazy? Took up a new crusade, slicing bits off businessmen?'

Stranded in the centre of the floor, without his crutch, Eamon cut a pitiful figure. Robby almost felt sorry for him, until he heard the hate surge back into his voice. It was the only defence Eamon knew.

'Them bloody businessmen don't deserve any better. They've the country sold out, haven't they? To Europe, to the Brits. They've no morals ....'

'And Razor has? *You* have?' Robby shouted. 'My father had? Four to one, Eamon! That was fair, that was *moral*, was it?'

'You won't even go to his grave,' Eamon said, his face twisted to a grimace. 'You're not worthy of him. You're not worthy of this house, this land. You're not fit to be called a Wade.'

Robby stalked out into the yard. The sickening irony of it all was that he would never have been called a Wade if it hadn't been for his great-uncle. Grace had wanted Sean's name on Robby's birth certificate; but she and Sean hadn't married, and that had caused complications. She had had letters from him that spoke of 'our baby', and witnesses to his excitement at the thought of becoming a father. The one thing she hadn't had was the money to take this evidence into court. But Eamon had wanted the Wade name for Robby as much as Grace had — and he had paid all the legal costs. He'd bought Robby a name, and now he wanted it back.

Bending down, Robby picked up a handful of earth from the old flowerbed below the window. It was dry from the summer heat. His fingers dug deeper, to where the clay was damp, and gouged out a great lump of it.

Eamon had managed to get back to his chair. Robby thrust his fist to within inches of Eamon's face.

'See that?' he spat. 'I don't want one grain of that muck.

Soon as I get the money together, I'm going over to England.
Yeah, England! And you can feed yourself, and do your
own messages, and dig your own drains and herd your
own cattle. And you can stuff your lousy little kingdom.'

He dropped the lump of clay on Eamon's plate and
left.

ся

'Can I help you?' Mayfly asked the big, bedraggled stranger.

'Any chance of a cup of tea, Miss?' His lowered eyes
seemed momentarily shifty, but the weariness in his voice
disarmed her. 'I'm parched.'

An hour had passed since she'd left Rusty at the cottage. She needed to get back there, but first she had to go
into town to buy bamboo shoots for the herbal mix. The
other ingredients were used in cooking, so she already
had plenty of them.

As the stranger gazed tiredly at the stone circle in its
high place, Mayfly saw in him something of the future
Bubble: older, alone, still on the run from reality, his face
pitted and weathered as ancient tree-bark.

'Do you drink herbal tea? Peppermint? Camomile?'

He looked up at her and laughed, pulling at his ear
shyly, his eyes wide with a manic surprise.

'Ah God, no, Miss. A drop of milk'd be grand.'

'Soya milk? I'm afraid that's all we have,' she said,
amused at his confusion. 'We do have coffee. Would that
be all right?'

'That'd be fine. I don't want to be troubling you, now,
mind.'

'I'll put the kettle on,' Mayfly said. 'I'd ask you in, only
my mum's resting.'

The stranger was already making himself comfortable
on the roadside grass.

'Not at all,' he said. 'Aren't I grand out here, hah?'

When Mayfly came back out of the dormobile, the man

had stretched himself out on the rich pile of warm grass as though to sleep; but Mayfly saw that one eyelid was slightly raised, the pupil alert and searching.

'If you don't mind, Miss, I think I'll leave the coffee.' He grinned, showing bad, unwashed teeth, and clambered to his feet, more agile than she'd expected him to be. 'Wouldn't be my cup of tea at all, the old coffee.'

'But it's no trouble, really,' Mayfly said. Just then, she saw Bubble sauntering in from the main road.

'Ah, no. I'll move along. Not meaning to be ungrateful, but I've some friends up the way here,' the stranger said, already on his way. 'Thanks all the same. You're a decent skin, Miss.'

Mayfly watched the hunched figure retreat, taking with him whatever sympathy she was capable of feeling at that moment. If Bubble ended up a lonely wanderer, it would be his own fault. Life had given him every chance, but he'd gone his own foolish way — and dragged Andy and Mayfly with him.

Bubble was picking wildflowers. He chose them slowly, as if from a market stall: daisies, buttercups, foxgloves, a spray of whitethorn from the hedge. Flicking the grey dreadlocks away from his face, he arranged the tiny bouquet carefully and considered it, changing a flower here, a stem there.

There was a time when the scene would have delighted Mayfly. Now, it maddened her.

It seemed a very long time ago that Bubble had been the light of her life — more so even than Andy, perhaps, if Mayfly was to be honest. Bubble, slightly dishevelled but always somehow elegant, his handsome face tanned with leathery creases, his eyes a shade of blue she'd never seen in any other person. Lapis lazuli, Andy called it. The colour reminded Mayfly of bright distances and seemed to reflect Bubble's quiet reserve. He always gave the impression that he found it easier to sing than to talk. His voice was deep and soothing as he played the old Bob Dylan songs Andy loved — 'Forever Young', 'Don't Think Twice, It's All Right', 'The Times They Are A-Changing' ....

'Who was that guy?' he asked, all sunny and beaming with satisfaction — at the prospect of the hash in his pocket, no doubt.

'Some traveller. I was making him coffee, but it looks like you scared him off.'

Bubble held out the flowers. 'For you.'

'Give them to Andy.'

'I'd like you to have them,' he said. 'A peace offering.'

When Mayfly raised her hand, he misunderstood and tried to give the little bouquet to her. She brushed it aside.

'I need some money. Two or three pounds,' she said. 'If you've any left.'

Bubble didn't try to persuade her any further. The hand grasping the flowers fell to his side. With the other hand, he fished out some pound coins. Then he changed his mind and gave her a fiver, so frayed that its silver strip hung loose like a shred of tinsel.

'Thanks.'

'Can we call a truce until ... until later?'

'What about the stones?' Mayfly enquired unpleasantly. 'What about the big miracle?'

'It could happen. It *will* happen.'

'There's a No Trespassing sign in that field,' she said, casting aside Andy's plea for togetherness. 'And I've already been warned off — at gunpoint. You won't get to prance around the stones. What then?'

He crushed the flowers to a mess of burst petals and split stems. The breeze was too slight to carry them far, and they fell like confetti at his feet.

Taking possession of the stones with his gaze, he said, 'Let them stop me. Just let them try, man.'

chapter 6

Nature's Delight, the health-food shop which Mayfly had been directed to, lay at the far end of the shopping-centre mall. The assistant, a young fair-haired girl, didn't look particularly delighted with herself. Mayfly asked for bamboo shoots and the girl muttered, with an aggravated sigh, 'I'm only minding the shop. If they're not on the shelves, I suppose we don't have them.'

While she searched among the shelves, Mayfly became aware of a uniformed man staring in at her between the posters on the shop window. Well used to suspicious attention, she ignored him. She found the bamboo shoots and took them to the counter. The bored assistant regarded the frayed fiver derisively. With growing impatience, Mayfly watched her puzzle out the change.

Against her better instincts, she glanced at the security man, who had moved to the door to get a clearer view of her. He was short and overweight, and his thick lips mouthed into a walkie-talkie. His peaked military-style hat was too small for his cropped head. Her calculations finally concluded, the assistant dropped some coins on the counter, ignoring Mayfly's outstretched hand.

When Mayfly emerged from the shop, the man followed her. The reflection of his arrogant little strut slid greasily along the shop-fronts. With every step, Mayfly's concern for Rusty lost its immediacy. In its place a foolish indignation reared up and took possession of her.

Near the entrance lobby was a large open-plan clothing section. Mayfly wandered in among the racks of blouses and skirts. When she was sure her stalker was nearby, she dawdled by a shelf of gloves. She tried on a black leather pair. Clipped together with a plastic tag, they felt like soft handcuffs. Suddenly she ducked down, left the gloves on the floor and stuffed the brown paper bag of bamboo shoots under her cardigan. Then she stepped out into the shop's central aisle and walked directly towards the security man, making no effort to hide the bulge at her side.

'Where do you think you're going?' he demanded.

'Are you talking to me, Sergeant?' Mayfly asked, giving him a mock salute. 'Or is it Captain? Or General?'

'What's that under your cardigan?' He pointed a damp, chubby finger at her side.

'I'm expecting a baby. She moves around a lot.'

'Right, you're coming with me,' he said, grabbing her wrist. 'To the manager's office.'

ᛊ

Whenever Robby ventured into town these days, he took the long way round, so as to avoid his mother's new home. Three months had passed since he'd been in that house, and he also steered clear of O'Neill's small garage. Grace and Liam had driven out to the farm several times in the previous weeks, and each time, Robby had got Eamon to tell them he wasn't in. Eamon didn't mind disappointing them. But he relayed mysterious messages: 'Tell him it's important'; 'We really have to see him' ....

As Robby turned down the side-street towards the shopping centre, his argument with Eamon filled his thoughts. All that stuff about going to England had come off the top of his head. Even as he'd blurted it out, he'd known it was crazy. Go to England? At seventeen, with nothing in his pockets — not even his Leaving Cert. results? He'd heard of fellows who'd done that and ended up in all kinds of trouble. Besides, he didn't like cities any more than he liked small towns.

He headed for the new music shop at the centre. In his

pocket he had thirty pounds of birthday money from his mother; he hadn't refused it because he couldn't afford to. Eamon gave him the odd fiver now and again, but he always made a big deal of it, never acknowledging the fact that Robby did most of the work. Not that Robby minded work. There was no better way to clear his head than to climb onto the roof of the barn and get busy with a hammer and nails, or wander around the farm looking for gaps in the hedges to make good. While Robby worked, Eamon made all the decisions — all of them bad.

They were down to twenty cattle; the barn was a rusty, shaking shambles; the tractor was a museum piece; the sky-blue Cortina, which Eamon wouldn't let Robby drive except on the farm lane, was equally decrepit. But all that hardly mattered now. Robby knew where he stood with Eamon. *Not a Wade. Not worthy ....*

There was, of course, the offer of a job at O'Neill's garage. But that was a compromise Robby could never accept. And the New Age life? A pipe dream, unattainable as the girl in the green dress who'd taken Rusty from him as easily as a toy from a child. If he ever took to the road, he'd be more likely to end up like Tommy the Tramp.

The shopping-centre doors slid apart. Robby saw the wild waves of red hair and the green dress, surrounded by a crowd. Then he heard her voice echo through the mall.

'Get your filthy hands off me!'

'Come on, move it,' the security guard warned.

'Airhead! Fascist!' Enraged at the unexpected turn her prank had taken, Mayfly meant her insults as much for herself as for the man twisting her arm behind her back. Rusty was surely dead by now, and if so she was to blame. Couldn't help a poisoned dog, never mind .... 'You fascist pig, you're hurting me! You're *hurting* me!'

'Start walking before I do some real damage to your arm, you little knacker.'

Suddenly the pressure was released and Mayfly broke free. Standing a head over the security man, tapping the broad, uniformed chest, was the young gunman from Cloghercree. His face betrayed a dark intensity that had been absent earlier, even as he'd threatened her.

'Lay off her, right?' he warned.

'Stay out of this, Wade,' the stout man warned. He stepped back, calling urgently into the walkie-talkie. 'Mick, get over here fast. Front of the clothes store. It's one of the Wades from Cloghercree.'

Robby caught Mayfly's eye and motioned to her to make her escape through the gathering throng.

'I can fight my own corner, thank you very much,' Mayfly said. 'Action Man.'

'You weren't making much of a fist of it, were you?' Robby answered.

'Did you bring your gun with you, Action Man?'

The spectators, who'd been drawing closer, began to retreat. 'A gun!' someone whispered melodramatically. Between Mayfly and Robby, the security guard squawked another panicky plea into his crackling walkie-talkie.

'For Jaysus' sake, Mick, would you hurry up,' he said, but there was no answering radio cackle. Considering his chances of survival, he backed away through the few shoppers brave enough to wait around for the finale.

'Get out of here, Wade, and take her with you,' he yelped. 'Or I'll call the guards.'

Robby was ten yards behind when Mayfly reached the exit without looking back. The clammy weight of the unnecessary heat in the shopping centre bore down upon him. All the miserable futility of his arguments with Eamon and with Liam O'Neill, all the angry silences of those interludes with his mother, the thought of Rusty's pain, the niggling fear that Razor McCabe might yet come to Cloghercree — all of these things pushed him over the edge of his usual reticence.

'Thanks for saying thanks,' he said, loudly enough for her to hear over the whoosh of the sliding doors.

A spasm of tension gripped Mayfly between the shoulder-blades as he followed her outside.

'How's my dog?' he called. 'Is he still alive?'

'Yes, he is,' Mayfly snapped. 'Least he's not riddled with bullet holes.'

'I wasn't trying to be cruel for the fun of it. I've had that dog all my life.'

'Thou shalt not kill. Didn't anyone ever teach you that? Or are the rules different here?'

Robby shrugged, and Mayfly mistook his silence for uncaring nonchalance.

'Mr Action-Man Wade,' she went on. 'Into guns in a big way, the Wades, are they?'

'You could say that,' Robby said.

'You could say da'.' Mayfly repeated his words in a poor imitation of his flat Midlands accent. 'Think you're cool, don't you?'

'No.'

In Mayfly's exasperation, Bubble's idea of circling the stones at Cloghercree became a cause to her, to be defended against this irritating native.

'Think you can stop us from going up to that stone circle, with your gun and your dumb sign? Well, watch this space, Action Man.'

'Not me. I don't care if you dance naked around it,' he told her. 'But if you do, cover your butt. My great-uncle's a better shot than I am.'

 ## chapter 7

Robby made a habit of walking home along the wrong side of the Cloghercree Road. Usually he was careful to dodge onto the grass verge when cars sped up behind him, but on this June evening he let the drivers worry about the dodging. Sometimes they blasted their horns impatiently as they went by. His answer was a one-fingered wave. He'd delivered three such greetings by the time he reached the cemetery. It lay on the other side of the road, the wrought-iron gates closed and padlocked, as if anyone would want to break in there. He passed by, his eyes fixed on the road ahead.

At the brow of the rising road stood the cracked pillars of the farm entrance. The long evening lay before him like another hill to be climbed. He was sorry he hadn't gone back into the music store. At least then he might have had something new to listen to on his Walkman.

The yellow and pink van was still parked on the back road. Chances were Eamon would have seen it by now, perhaps even already have gone to warn the travellers off. This, and the fact that Robby was so late — not to speak of what had happened earlier between them — would have Eamon's blood pressure shooting sky-high.

Robby turned in at the entrance and saw a squad car making its bumpy way down the lane from the house. More trouble. He half-expected to see Eamon scowling at him from the back seat.

The white Sierra slowed as it approached. Healy's aggressive young companion was its only occupant. He looked at Robby as though he were some particularly repellent specimen in a zoo. Robby didn't react, and the car passed him with a screech of wheels and a cloud of dust. At least the guards' continuing attentions made it more unlikely that McCabe would risk hiding out in Cloghercree.

The large house, standing sideways on to the road, was dwarfed by the giant crescent of oak and beech trees surrounding it. Along the chimney block jutting out from the gable end, a long, snaking crack widened in the greenish-grey plaster. Rising two storeys above a base-ment whose bricked-up windows seemed to emerge half-formed from the ground, the place had a sunken look. It looked into the trees with an air of empty pride, as if recalling a past that had been more glorious — before the Wades arrived.

Robby went through the arch in the burnished red-brick wall to the rear of the house. The cobbles of the yard were buried under layers of straw, cow-dung and weeds. This soft covering absorbed the sound of his footsteps, which was useful on those rare occasions when he stayed out late, invariably alone, at the cinema or one of the local night spots.

The back door stood open and, inside, Eamon sat at his usual place by the fire. Not a single cup had been re-moved from the kitchen table since Robby had left. The plateful of clay turned his stomach, and he headed for the door to the hallway.

'Did you eat?' Eamon asked, in his familiar hurt tone.

'I had a burger and chips at the Mona Lisa.' The door moved heavily on its hinges. Like all the doors in the ancient house, it was worthy of any prison.

'More than I had,' Eamon said. 'They came again. The guards. That snotty little pup that was here earlier.'

Robby leaned against the door-jamb. The cold draught from the hallway, which was always dark, chilled him.

'What did he want?'

'Well, he wasn't selling raffle tickets, was he?' Eamon muttered. 'I told him he'd be better off searching those knackers for drugs.'

'Knackers? Where?' Robby asked, feigning disinterest.

'On the back road. Pulled in during the day. Only for them bloody guards coming round here day and night, I'd fire a few shots over those mangy hippie heads of theirs. They'd soon be hopping away out of here then. I might just do it yet, before they start fecking stuff left, right and centre.'

'We don't have anything worth stealing,' Robby said.

He took a step into the hallway. Even as a child, he'd been filled with dread in that night-shadowy, cavernous space. Since he'd come to live in the house, two years before, and the haunting dream had begun, the impression of disturbed spirits had returned.

'Robby?' Eamon followed him to the foot of the stairs, his stick knocking sharply on the tiled floor.

'I'm going up to listen to some music.'

'I know, but ... there's something I wanted to say ....'

An apology? From Eamon? Hardly likely. No, it was McCabe. He was going to announce Razor McCabe's arrival. Halfway up the steps, Robby paused, his expression hard with resentment.

'I wanted to say that maybe ... maybe you should call in to your mother. She's fierce anxious about you.'

'I bet she is,' Robby answered evenly, but he was taken aback.

'She is, now. In fairness.'

'What does she want? To tell me something, is it?' He looked closely at Eamon for some sign. On the night of the big argument, Grace had said something about being better off a million miles from this country. 'They're moving away.'

Eamon seemed genuinely surprised at the suggestion. 'No, she's only anxious you mightn't be talking to her any more, maybe.'

'You never worried about her before.'

Even with the stick, Eamon could never stand in one position for very long. He held on to the carved wooden ball of the banister. His mood was darkening, as though he too was discomfited by the ghostly air of the hallway.

'There was a time when I worried about nothing else,' he said. 'Look, I'm fed up of making excuses for you. They're out here morning, noon and night, looking for you.'

'They were here today?'

'No, but I don't want them around the place. Not now.'

The real cause of Eamon's concern was just what Robby had suspected. He descended the stairs to stand beside his great-uncle.

'Right. *Not now*, because Razor McCabe might be along at any minute. Yeah?'

'I told you, Robby, he won't come next nor near us,' Eamon said. 'I got the word out on the grapevine that we're being hassled by the guards.'

'There's no problem, then, is there? And you don't have to make any excuses. Just tell them to shag off.'

Choking on his words, Robby climbed the stairs into the greater darkness above. As he crossed the landing and went out of Eamon's view, his great-uncle shouted upwards into the vaultlike recesses, 'For God's sake, Robby, will you keep O'Neill away from here! If — if, by some chance, McCabe .... There's a fierce bitterness there, Robby. Razor could lose the head altogether if he saw him.'

Robby peered down into the well of the murky hallway. His great-uncle's face looked misshapen and unreal, as though painted by some mediaeval artist capturing the agonies of hell.

# chapter 8

All four rings of the dormobile's gas cooker spouted purple flames that hungrily licked the blackened pots. In one pot was the vegetable curry, in another the whole-grain rice, and a third contained lentil soup. But the pot to which Mayfly paid most attention was the one in which Rusty's herbal infusion simmered. Out on the lane, Bubble combed the hedges for firewood, while Andy sat, humming to herself, by the pile of twigs and broken branches he'd gathered so far. As Mayfly left for the cottage, the air of industry and contented quiet that pervaded the camp was almost like happiness.

The muddy brown mixture lapped over onto her hands as she went, sending splashes onto her green dress. Rusty's plaintive whines could be heard twenty yards from the cottage, and that worried her. If the dark young gunman wandered too near, as he patrolled his precious fields, he'd surely hear the dog. He or his great-uncle — the better shot.

At first, the liquid spilled from Rusty's mouth as though he no longer had the energy to swallow. Then, as Mayfly spooned in some more, he gagged and coughed it back up, spattering her face. Mayfly persisted, and finally he gulped down spoon after spoon of the stuff. The effort exhausted him. His body went limp, his eyes glazed over. For one terrible moment, Mayfly imagined that she'd given him too much and that her supposed cure had killed him. She waited, and the gasping rhythm of his breath returned.

There was no more she could do for the present and,

back at the dormobile, the dinner was probably just about ready.

Dusk had begun to fall and, in the distance, the bright end of the sky glowed with pinky-orange promise. Outside the dormobile, Bubble had the fire going. Sparks flew upwards among the swirls of white smoke which gave off a sharp, fruity smell. Andy swayed to some inner music. Her face, vividly alive in the flames' soft light, radiated a warm serenity. Unjust the world might be, but it still had the power to transform. Mayfly was determined that this night there would no truculence, no thinly-veiled expressions of blame, no dwelling on fearful imaginings.

'How's your patient, Fly?' Bubble called out.

'Great,' Mayfly said, willing herself to be equable. 'Well, he's alive, anyway.'

Well used to the cramped working-space in Nirvana, Mayfly dished out the food expertly and carried the bowls and plates down the steps from the dormobile without spilling a drop or morsel. Bubble and Andy talked incessantly while they ate, and it was all talk of the past. The herbs had reminded Andy of the Californian commune where she'd learned how to grow and use them. Mayfly allowed herself to savour her mother's recovery from the tiring journey. Even Bubble's interruptions failed to annoy her. They looked as young, in the firelight's complimentary glow, as in the collage of photos on her compartment wall. Around them, the night's cold air was no match for the heat of the campfire, or for its kindliness.

The outline of hills surrounding Cloghercree was only barely visible when they finished eating. The ditches resounded with the syncopated ticking of crickets. Out on the main road, cars came and went.

'Good times, Andy,' Bubble said quietly.

'Sure were,' she said. Then, reaching to take Mayfly's hand, she declared, 'But these, these are good times too, right? Just feel this night. Look at that moon up there and tell me this is not a good time.'

They looked. The moon, not yet full, had a faint blue-grey crescent on its left side. On its cream-cheese surface, every porelike crater was visible.

'And the stones over there,' Andy went on. 'Look what the moon's done to the stones.'

The stone circle was transformed. No longer a mere jagged outcrop, it shone like a softly lit stage. So stunning was the sight that Mayfly could almost believe in Bubble's crazy scheme. Until he spoke.

'Another hour, Andy, and we'll be up there. You're not too tired, are you?'

'At midnight?' Mayfly objected. 'You want to go there at midnight? And after that awful journey?'

'I'm fine, Mayfly. Don't worry. Bubble's got it all worked out. Tell her, Bubble.'

'I think I'd better check on the dog,' Mayfly said, but her mother's grip was too tight.

Somewhat embarrassedly, conscious of his daughter's scepticism, Bubble spelled out the details.

'See, these stones — they were placed very precisely, to tap the energies that control the inner balance of the earth, of the stars. Energies that heal. These stone circles are everywhere — Europe, Asia, North America. Cloghercree is special because its stone circle is the closest to the very centre of the island of Ireland. And Ireland's special ... well, because I had this dream about a stone circle and I knew it was in Ireland.'

Mayfly looked into the flames. The logic of their journey was even flakier than she'd imagined.

'And this was a mystical time for the people who built the circles. In three days, we've got Midsummer's Eve — shortest night of the year. And they had mystical numbers, too: the number three and the number seven. So, each night for the next three nights, we walk around the stones seven times and repeat that three times, and ....'

Mayfly had had enough. She eased her hand from Andy's and stood up.

'I'm worried about the dog,' she said. 'I should go.'

'You'll be back before midnight, won't you?' Andy asked.

Mayfly couldn't bring herself to look at her mother. The fire had been neglected, and Bubble was just the middle-aged, grey-dreadlocked Bubble again. She was afraid Andy would seem old again too, and sickly.

Mayfly took a torch from the cab of the dormobile. Facing towards the cottage, she tested it. Shadows darted in the flash of wavering light, evoking a sense of small, frightened things, escaping, hiding. She switched off the torch to save the batteries and headed for the cottage.

chapter 9

Robby hadn't heard the car arrive in the yard, nor Eamon's hurried footsteps on the stairs. In his room, he lay on the bed, his eyes closed, the headphones of his Walkman in place. Jeff Buckley's plaintive, almost ghostly singing was exactly suited to his mood. The dead singer's young voice felt like Robby's own.

The bedroom door flew open. Eamon's worried lips moved, but Robby heard only a low mutter below the music. Reluctantly he pulled off the headphones. From Eamon's panicked features, he expected to hear that Razor McCabe had arrived after all. What he heard seemed, for a moment, infinitely worse. His mother and Liam O'Neill were waiting for him down in the kitchen.

'They won't leave until they see you,' Eamon said. 'Get it over with, will you, Robby? McCabe won't come, but if he does .... For your mother's sake, go down.'

Robby steeled himself to face whatever bad news they'd come to deliver. And of course it would be bad news. Good news was never surrounded with such urgency.

Descending the stairs, he heard his great-uncle's bedroom door close and was even more disturbed to hear the key turn in the lock. Eamon never locked his door.

In the kitchen, Grace sat by the fire, in Eamon's grubby armchair. She'd changed her hair. The blonde waves were cut to a neat crop which made her look younger than ever. The brown suede jacket and short black skirt completed the impression of youth. Grace was thirty-five, but she could easily have passed for a sister to Robby.

Liam O'Neill stood close by, warming his hands behind

him. Track-suited and fit — and still lining out on the local hurling team — he bristled with health and energy. The slight touch of grey in his shock of carrot-red hair was the only sign that he'd aged since Robby had last seen him.

'How are you, Robby?' Grace asked nervously. 'Like my new look?'

'Yeah, it's all right,' Robby said, not moving from the doorway.

'Working hard, yeah?' O'Neill enquired. 'You're not an easy man to find.'

It wasn't until Robby had begun to show his dislike of O'Neill that he'd noticed the raw, impatient edge to his character. The eight years O'Neill had spent in a Northern Ireland prison — braving, all the while, the hostility of the former IRA friends he'd parted company with — had no doubt contributed to this steeliness.

'Well, I'm here now,' he said. 'To talk to my mother.'

Robby sat at the kitchen table, O'Neill at the second fireside chair, beside Rusty's basket. Earlier, Robby had listened at the open window of his room for some indication that his dog was still alive. Hearing none, he'd been tempted to go to the oddly coloured van, but he knew he couldn't face the girl again.

'Robby,' Grace said nervously. 'We're going on a holiday to Kenmare, down in Kerry, and we'd like you to come. Wouldn't we, Liam?'

Liam nodded in assent, but Robby made no response.

'We've a house booked for the first two weeks of July,' Grace continued desperately, 'and there's lots of room. You will come, won't you? You need a break from' — she surveyed the kitchen with distaste — 'from all this.'

'There's a lot of stuff to be done here,' Robby said. 'And Eamon's not up to it.'

O'Neill shifted in his seat. 'It wasn't just your mother's idea, Robby,' he said, as deceptively soft-spoken as ever. 'We need to get things sorted out between us, all three of us.'

'You think so? Well, I don't —'

'Robby,' Grace broke in. 'You'd like it. The sea's only a few hundred yards from the house, and there's a TV with the satellite channels ....' Her hands moved jerkily, like the hands of the smoker she had once been, craving a cigarette.

'Grace, I don't think he —' O'Neill began.

'You have no idea what I think,' Robby muttered.

In spite of Grace's beseeching glance, O'Neill got up and moved towards Robby. Robby stood three or four inches taller than his mother's husband, but it didn't feel like any advantage. O'Neill walked past him with a deadpan look that betrayed no emotion, least of all fear.

'I told you this wouldn't work, Grace,' O'Neill said. 'You'll have to talk to him yourself. I'm sorry.' A cold draught pushed its way in from the yard as he went outside.

Robby's legs felt weak, and he held on to the table.

'Talk to me about what, Mam?'

Grace lowered her head and ran her knuckles roughly along her lips, as if wiping away some unwelcome taste.

'Sit over here,' she pleaded. 'Robby, don't do this to me. Don't make it any harder. Sit beside me.'

'You're going to live somewhere else,' he said.

It was easy to hate her when she wasn't around, but in her presence he felt only how much he missed her. He sat by the fire, letting the chair slide back so that her hands couldn't reach him.

'No, we're not moving anywhere.'

'So what's the big mystery, then?'

'Robby, this is difficult .... It shouldn't be, but .... Listen, Robby, this won't change anything between us ....'

The fire was too warm, her eyes too fearful, the space between them too empty. He wanted her to say what was on her mind. He wanted her not to say what was on her mind.

'I'm going to have a baby, Robby.'

Instinctively, Robby looked at her stomach and then turned away in embarrassed confusion. He couldn't take it in. She didn't even look pregnant. She couldn't start all over again without him. Not with O'Neill. Not with anyone.

He tried to smile. His lower lip danced like there was a nerve in there gone mad.

'I'm three months gone,' Grace said. 'I've been wanting to tell you so much.'

She leaned forward, and Robby pushed his chair back until Rusty's basket got in the way. He heard the frayed strands of the wicker basket straining, cracking, breaking.

'That's why I want you to be with us, Robby. I should never have let you stay here with Eamon. But I didn't know what to do. I thought you'd come back to me. I handled it all so badly. I'm sorry, Robby, I really am. But please don't blame Liam. He didn't want to leave you here.'

Robby couldn't bear to look at her any more — at the fancy new hairstyle, the teenage clothes, the slight bump pushing out the waistline of her short skirt. He didn't want to imagine what Eamon would say when he found out.

'You know I loved your father. But he was only nineteen, Robby. I was eighteen. And I'm not eighteen any more. Time passes. I used to blame Eamon for putting all those ideas into Sean's head, about going up north to fight. But he didn't need persuading. I know that now. He was a dreamer, but he dreamed the wrong dream. He was just a muddle-headed kid, like I was. Except that I was lucky enough to grow a bit older. And I was lucky enough to have you to see me through.'

Just a muddle-headed kid? That explained it all, did it? Muddle-headedness might explain an obsession with some grand cause. But to deliberately lie in wait to kill another human being called for a cold, clear determination. Robby feared that coldness, that icy detachment, and he feared it all the more because he sometimes felt it in himself. He felt it as his mother spoke.

'We can be a family, the four of us. Can you imagine? A little kid to boss around, Robby.'

He rose from his chair like someone who had somewhere urgent to go to. He didn't; he was trapped more firmly than ever in Cloghercree. He'd never share a life with O'Neill or his child.

'At least,' he said, 'it won't be someone's little bastard, like I was.'

He couldn't believe what he'd said. He stood helplessly as Grace swept by him, crying, fumbled blindly with the door and ran outside.

Faintly lit by the kitchen lights, O'Neill emerged from his flashy red Toyota and made for the door. Robby sprang forward and almost got it closed, but O'Neill jammed his trainer at the base, keeping it open a few inches. His face was livid and his body, pressed against the door, shook with rage.

'What did you say to her?' he demanded.

'That's none of your business.'

'You've no right to go upsetting her. In her condition.'

'You put her in that *condition*, O'Neill.'

The door timbers protested creakingly at the renewed pressure from both sides. Robby held firm.

'Don't come near us any more. Do you hear me?'

'Why don't you grow up, Robby? Let your mother have a life, even if you don't have the cop-on to get one for yourself.'

O'Neill stopped pushing the door, but kept his foot as a block. He looked as though he already regretted what he'd said, but the last thing Robby wanted was O'Neill's regret.

'Get lost, O'Neill. Go back to Donegal or whatever hole you crawled out of.'

'This is crazy, Robby,' O'Neill said. 'We were good friends, you and me.'

'You used me to get Grace, that was all. Played up to the young lad. Made it easy to move in on her.'

'Do you really think it was easy for me to admit, even to myself, that I loved your mother, Robby? Do you think it was easy for her to admit that she loved me?'

'Just go. Stay away from Cloghercree. You have her now. Soon you'll have your little family. What more do you want from me?'

'Things will never be right between your mother and me while you're with Eamon. She's half out of her mind worrying he'll lead you astray.'

'But she's not worried that you'd lead me astray, O'Neill? Since when were you such a holy innocent?'

'A man can change, Robby.'

'You can't change what you did,' Robby said. 'Now leave me alone. Stay away from Cloghercree.'

O'Neill slowly withdrew his foot, all the while staring at Robby, curious, questioning.

'Why do you keep saying that, Robby? "Stay away from Cloghercree"?'

'Because you make me sick every time I look at you.' Subdued by O'Neill's quizzical gaze, Robby could summon no ferocity into his voice.

'Yeah, yeah, we all know that. But this is different.'

'It's not different.'

'Robby, has this something to do with McCabe?' O'Neill whispered.

'Oh yeah, he's inside waiting to have a chat with you, O'Neill. He's only dying to meet you, reminisce about old times above in Fermanagh.'

He slammed the door in O'Neill's face and slumped against it. Listening to the car starting up and pulling slowly away, he pressed his folded arms to his stomach, holding on, holding it all in.

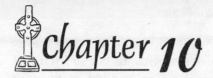

chapter 10

The beam from the torch, which Mayfly had placed among the debris on the mantelpiece, flickered and wavered. She spooned more of the herbal brew into Rusty. Her touch drew no response from the dog's rigid body, but the liquid went down. She covered him again and went to switch off the torch. Then she opened the makeshift curtain she'd placed across the back window. Pale moonlight filtered inwards. She sat beside Rusty, her back resting against the wall.

Her efforts had calmed her down, but Bubble's proposed ritual still played on her mind. Hard as she tried to be tolerant, he had the knack of always pushing her too far. Had he no idea how exhausted Andy must be? And he expected her to walk around those stones, not once, as Mayfly had imagined, but twenty-one times? The very recollection of the day's journey tired her. They'd left the site outside Birmingham at three o'clock in the morning; at seven, after a two-hour wait at Holyhead, the ferry had set off. Three hours later they'd arrived in Dun Laoghaire, and then there had been the long drive to this remote place.

She ceased resisting the fall of her heavy eyelids. Before her, images of the day came and went as though she were leafing slowly through an album of photos. The stone circle, seen from the approach road; her mother's fleeting look of concern — had Andy really been just remembering a bad dream, or had it been a premonition? Action Man with his gun; the travelling man; Bubble's wildflowers; the uniformed shopping-centre fascist; Action Man without his gun. She slept.

She was surrounded by the crash of waves, gusts of windswept rain, a thud of far-off thunder, a sudden lull. Then those waves again, and a louder snap of thunder. Mayfly woke with a start. The long rectangle of moonlight on the floor at her feet bore the shadow of a floating figure. In an instant, the shadow had disappeared.

The whooshing sounds started up again. Not waves, nor rain, but disturbed undergrowth.

Close at hand lay the broken leg of a kitchen chair. She picked it up. She waited, following the shadow's invisible but noisy progress as it circled the cottage towards the front door.

CஒB

Robby lay in a hospital bed, unable to move. All was white — the ceiling, the lampshade, the glass of the bright bulb. He could see only the top of the window opposite the bed. Its drawn curtain was white too. Beyond that he could see no more, except for a thin strip of white wall on each side of the window. But there were voices, low murmurings, incoherent words. All he knew was that they were expressions of concern for him. He couldn't distinguish the individual voices, but he knew who was in the ward: Eamon, Liam O'Neill, Grace, his father. And a new presence: the New Age girl. Of them, he saw only insubstantial shadows on the ceiling, ebbing and flowing like clouded light on water.

He felt no pain, only an unbearable sadness, a longing he was incapable of expressing even in the form of a solitary tear. It would always be like this, never ending until the darkness finally fell and their voices receded from him for the rest of time, their lives going on as if he'd never existed. He couldn't blame them for that, but it still felt like betrayal.

Then, knowing it was useless, he began to struggle again — tried to move his head, his eyes, his lips, tried to force some sound out. He focused his efforts on his arms; then, with growing terror, on his wrists, his hands, his fingers, one small finger. Nothing moved, and the scream he knew no one could hear echoed in his head. 'Let me die, please, let me die' — and he woke.

He sat up, swept off his sweat-soaked T-shirt and flung it across towards the high chest of drawers. The chill of the old house spread over his back instantly. On his knees, he went along the bed and reached for the drawer where he kept his clean gear. The loosely swinging handle of the drawer rattled, and Robby thought he heard a sudden movement from Eamon's bedroom at the front of the house. He listened, but there was only the muffled turning of the springs in the grandfather clock on the landing.

When he'd pulled the fresh T-shirt over his head, he was facing the window. The night was clear — clear enough for him to see a lone figure standing at the stone circle. He moved closer to the window, wiping away the fog of breath that blurred his view. Wiping away, too, it seemed, all trace of the intruder. He waited, sure he hadn't imagined what he'd seen.

೦೩

The cottage door scraped open and Mayfly lurked behind it, the carved chair-leg at the ready. The door eased inwards. The dark outline of a man's head appeared — a head bearing a mass of untidy dreadlocks.

'Mayfly,' her father whispered. Then, spotting the raised chair-leg, he whisked back out of sight, with a strangled, 'It's me. Bubble.'

'What are you doing, sneaking around like that?' she snapped furiously. 'You knew I was here. All you had to do was call me.'

'Sorry, Fly, I thought you might be asleep.'

'I was. Until you came skulking around.'

They were out on the front path, and Bubble was looking less optimistic than he had at the campfire.

'Yeah, well, I was thinking, you know, if you were sleeping, I wouldn't wake you,' he said.

'You were going to go without me?'

'I can't win with you, man,' he complained. 'I know you think it's a lot of nonsense. Now I say you don't have to come, and you accuse me of leaving you out.'

Mayfly tossed the chair-leg back into the pile of rags and old newspapers by the door and walked beside him.

'Wherever Andy goes, I go,' she told him. 'Someone has to take care of her.'

෫

When Robby saw, through the rivulets left by his finger-swipes, three people approaching the stones, his first reaction was relief. McCabe would certainly have been alone. These were the New Agers, he was sure of it. He'd have to warn them off. Eamon took badly enough to day-trippers; this night intrusion would really set him off.

Dressing quickly, he slid the window upwards and dropped down in his stockinged feet to the tiled roof of the toolshed. From there he made it to the yard, slipped his shoes on and skirted around to the barn. Once inside, he went to where the rifle was hidden.

The girl's nickname for him, Action Man, repeated itself like a schoolyard taunt as he edged back a pile of timber pallets. But while he slept, more of those New Agers might have gathered on the back road. After all, they travelled in convoys, didn't they? If there were only three, he could leave the gun in the ditch by the gate while he spoke to them.

The pallets removed, he kicked away the straw underneath and lifted the corrugated iron sheet below. The hempen flour-sack he drew out fell slack in his hand. The rifle wasn't there.

Then he remembered the key turning in Eamon's lock. Only he and Eamon knew where the rifle was hidden. Eamon had probably taken it to his room to protect himself — whether from McCabe or from the 'thieving hippies', Robby chose not to speculate. He replaced the covering of the hiding-place and hurried to the Stone Field.

છ

There were seven stones in the circle, not six as it had appeared from the back road. The seventh stone had fallen to the ground and was wrapped in swathes of grass. Bubble's declaration that this was a good omen, a confirmation of his theory of sacred numbers, left Mayfly cold. Any fool could see the irregular intervals between the stones and the empty post-holes, proving that originally there had been more than seven.

A low bank surrounded the circle, and in this man-made moat an entrance was gouged out. The stones varied in height. The largest, by the entrance, stood about five feet tall; the smallest, to the rear, less than three feet.

The midnight trek began, Bubble's arm supporting his wife. Their progress was torturously slow. Behind them, Mayfly was relieved that, at least, there was no chanting or dancing. She even managed a smile when she recalled Action Man's comment about covering her butt if they should go naked.

In spite of herself, the hope stirred irrationally within her that something extraordinary might really happen, and she struggled to contain fanciful imaginings of Andy's recovery.

She counted her paces, coming full circle at twenty-three. So much for Bubble's magic numbers. Twenty-three was a prime number, a number that couldn't be divided by anything but itself; and when you added or subtracted the two digits, you didn't get three or seven.

She tried the distraction of Rainbow Shades. The colour

she chose was purple, at the moon's suggestion — its shaded crescent had taken on a lavender hue. So, lavender. And lilac. Puce — 'the moon is puce', a phrase from some old song Bubble sang. Amethyst, magenta. Another circle completed, Mayfly looked about her for inspiration. The dark hills reminded her of heather, but did that qualify as a shade of purple? Or was it just ....

Her speculations ended abruptly. Unseen by Bubble and Andy, who were off on yet another circuit, Action Man was approaching the gate. He wasn't carrying a gun, but his haste was threatening in itself.

೮೩

Robby gripped the top rung of the gate and, in one leap, was over it. There were still three New Agers: a long-haired man and the woman in the white dress he'd seen earlier, walking hesitantly around the stones, followed by the girl. Some kind of freaky pagan ritual, he speculated, wondering what kind of weird bunch this was.

The couple halted at the entrance to the circle, and a male voice reverberated softly across the night meadow.

'There we go, then,' it said. 'That's twenty-one.'

The girl joined them, and all three turned towards Robby. He wished he'd stayed in his room and let Eamon sort them out in his own crude way. But he was there, across the circle from them, and he had to say something.

He addressed himself to the girl because he couldn't take his eyes off her.

'I asked you not to come up here.'

'You didn't *ask* me, you *warned* me.'

The couple looked on in growing surprise as the red-haired girl cut through the circle and advanced on Robby.

'I told you my great-uncle wouldn't like it. What are you doing, anyway?'

'Why aren't you tucked up in bed with your Action Man dollies?'

Behind her, the dreadlocked man followed the path she'd taken. Robby saw that his smile was conciliatory if not friendly.

'We don't mean any harm, man. It's not our intention to make a nuisance of ourselves.' The curious mix of hippie slang and plummy tones confused Robby.

'My great-uncle's very touchy about strangers on the land,' Robby said. 'Especially in the middle of the night.'

'A few days, man, and we'll be gone. That's not too much to ask, is it?'

'You lot always leave a mess after you. We have to live here. We have to clean up after you.'

'"You lot"? What's that supposed to mean?' the girl interjected. 'We've never been in these backwoods before.'

Robby glanced at her, then dispiritedly away. Even the bad dream was better than this, yet another of the constant confrontations which made up his life.

'I meant other — others like you ... other wasters,' he said, kicking at the standing stone before him, wishing he could kick harder.

'Now, listen here ....' the man objected. But a hand appeared at his shoulder, and the face of the woman in white hovered into view between him and the girl.

The girl's mother, surely. The resemblance was striking — the high cheekbones, the steep slant of the dark eyebrows, the slightly raised upper lip. But, if Robby was afraid to look into the girl's eyes, he couldn't resist the hypnotic effect of her mother's. Even before she'd moved close enough to take his hand, he felt as though he'd been touched. The woman was clearly very unwell, and yet she made him feel calmed.

'My name is Andy, short for Andrea,' she said, sounding to Robby like a laid-back country-and-western singer. 'This here is Bubble, my long-suffering partner. And our daughter, Mayfly. But I guess you've already met.'

'Yeah,' he replied, tongue-tied under the girl's tight-lipped glare.

'Aries, right?' Andy asked.

'Sorry?'

'Your star sign,' she explained. When he shrugged, she asked, 'When's your birthday? March? April?'

'March. The twenty-third.' He couldn't quite believe he was having this unlikely conversation in the Stone Field after midnight with all these oddly-named people, but he wasn't in any hurry for it to end.

'Sensitive, sincere, energetic,' she told him. 'But a bit of a tough guy hiding in there too, right?'

Inside the stone circle, Mayfly stood with folded arms and tossed her wild red hair impatiently. 'Hiding?' she snorted.

'Sometimes, you've got to be ... let's call it resilient. Right?' Andy said, and took hold of his hand. 'You haven't told us your name.'

'Robby. Robby Wade.' He withdrew his hand, only to have Bubble give it a firm thumbs-up handshake.

'Blenthyne. Bubble Blenthyne.'

'Mayfly,' Andy called. 'Come on over here.'

They shook hands briskly, across the barrier of the low standing stone. Robby found himself apologising again, but to Andy.

'It's my great-uncle, you see. He loses it when anyone comes up to the —'

'Tell you what we'll do, Robby,' she said. 'We'll take our chances with your great-uncle. You got your problems, we got ours, right? Let us worry about this one, OK? Deal?'

Robby knew he should feel offended at her offhand assumption that he had problems. Instead, he felt that she'd reached into his soul and that some inexplicable light had briefly shone there. The wisp of night air brought with it a pleasant shiver. There was no arguing with this woman and the firmness in her gentle certainty. He found himself regretting that she appeared so unhealthily fragile.

'Why did you come to Cloghercree?' he asked.

'The stones. See, we believe that the stones —' Bubble began.

'Bubble!' Mayfly exclaimed. 'You don't have to explain to him ....'

'Robby? Why don't you come to us for supper tomorrow evening and we'll talk about it?' Andy said. 'Say eight o'clock?'

ભ

Mayfly stormed away from the stone circle. She'd give him supper. Climbing through the hedge, she planned an extra-hot fire-and-brimstone curry that would have him racing back to his great-uncle in thirsty haste.

As she waited by Nirvana for her parents to emerge from the field, her rage subsided. The stillness of the night became a part of her being. The sense of calm that washed over her had nothing to do with peace or happiness. It was, rather, a tranquil prelude to the dawning of truth.

All day she'd been hiding behind a frenzy of rushing around to find a cure for Rusty, keeping busy with cooking and cleaning, venting her anger on the security guard and on Action Man and on Bubble. For weeks, months, she'd been carrying on like this.

The reasons were simple. She didn't want Andy to die. She was desperately afraid. She couldn't live without her.

But the real cause went deeper than that and had a harder, more unpalatable core to it. Achingly, almost sickeningly, Mayfly realised that, all along, she'd known her life wouldn't end when Andy's did.

Before her, the gap in the hedge, garlanded with a silhouette of leaves, was an empty frame.

CB

Robby went, smiling a little daftly, through the trees and past the barn. Even the girl's continuing hostility couldn't dull his sense of anticipation at the unexpected invitation. He didn't even bother to work on some foolproof excuse for going there. He'd think of something — say he was going into town or whatever.

If it had been daytime, he'd have been whistling contentedly as he entered the yard. If he'd been whistling, the melody would have wound down as tunelessly as a song on a Walkman with fading batteries. The kitchen light was on. Eamon would want to know why he'd left the house at such a late hour.

As he pushed the door open, he promised himself not to give any explanation. Why should he? He owed Eamon nothing.

In the fireplace, there was nothing left but the blackened stumps of burnt wood-blocks. Eamon sat there anyway, huddled up in his tartan dressing-gown, his feet, blue with cold, on the stone hearth.

'Where were you?' he asked. Robby kept walking towards the hallway door. 'Robby! Wait a —'

Robby swung the heavy door open and stood face to face with Razor McCabe.

Chapter 11

Mayfly had hated sleeping in the dormobile ever since Andy came out of hospital. Once, her mother had told her how frightened she'd been when the infant Mayfly slept. Night after night, she'd wake and place her hand near her daughter's tiny mouth to feel the barely-audible breath. Now, Mayfly's nights were punctuated with similar terrors. In her cramped compartment, she couldn't reach out for instant reassurance; she could only wait in growing fearfulness for her mother to breathe aloud again. Every hour held little deaths and temporary resurrections. As she washed up the dinner things in a plastic bucket at the sink, Mayfly knew she couldn't handle another night of it.

Out at the dying campfire, Bubble smoked his hash, losing himself in the stars. Behind Mayfly, Andy sat on the edge of the bed, drying the dishes in that painfully slow and fumbling way of hers. Reflected in the window above the sink, Andy's gaze met her daughter's across an immeasurable distance.

'Andy,' Mayfly said, 'I'm going to sleep in the cottage tonight, so's I can keep an eye on the dog. OK?'

Andy's dish-drying ground to a halt, as though she couldn't speak and work at the same time. 'Sure,' she said softly. 'And maybe tomorrow we can talk about what's going to happen to all of us. Make plans and stuff, right?'

'Right,' Mayfly said.

'Make the best sense we can of it all.'

'Right,' Mayfly repeated, and she thought that she could listen to whatever Andy had to say and not break down.

Then, as though Mayfly's earlier request had at last

registered with her, Andy asked, 'Are you sure you'll be
OK at the cottage?'

'Yeah, I'll be all right. I'll take my sleeping-bag.'

'And you'll sleep better there.'

There were no more pots to battle with, only the slops
in the plastic bucket to throw out. Mayfly heaved the
bucket from the sink and made for the door.

'It isn't that,' she said. 'I sleep fine here. I want to take
care of the dog, that's all.'

Finished with the dishes, Andy lay back on the bed
like a drowning woman giving herself up to the waves.
Mayfly opened the door. The campfire was a small red
glow, the flames a memory; Bubble sat there, no closer to
solving the sky's mysteries. She flung the soiled water
into the ditch and went back inside.

Below the white helmet of bandage, Andy's eyelids
flickered. Mayfly stood above her, careful not to let her
shadow fall across the pale, tired face. She wondered if in
her dreams Andy ever forgot she was dying. She hoped so.

But Andy wasn't sleeping yet. Mayfly stepped back
with a start when she spoke.

'Say good night to Bubble for me.'

Mayfly went into her compartment and pressed her
forehead to the icy, metallic wall until the bone ached
beneath her skin. She took the sleeping-bag from her bed
and rolled it up. Pausing on her way past Andy's bed, she
held out the palm of her hand an inch or so above her
mother's mouth. The warm breath moistened her skin.
She left the dormobile, her fist clenched as though she
held something of her mother there.

Bubble was nowhere to be seen. Off on one of his
midnight hikes, Mayfly supposed. He often wandered off
like that, when they travelled to new places, walking
along the roads and streets he'd been through during the
day. 'You get no sense of what a place is really like,' he

insisted, 'unless you've seen it in darkness and in light.'

The shadowy hedgerows were ugly, clawlike things as Mayfly neared the cottage. A vile smell of stale wood-smoke hung about her clothes and the sharp breeze reeked heavily of silage. The vulgar sounds of Rusty's agonies, coming from the cottage, almost tempted her to return to Nirvana. If he hadn't improved by morning, she'd bring Action Man to him. Robby. And his rifle.

ഗ

'Put it there, Robby boy. Any son of Sean Wade's is a friend of mine. Great lad, he was.'

Clean-shaven, his wet hair swept back from his fore-head, Razor McCabe was less unkempt than the television pictures had suggested. He was almost as tall as Robby, and his sleeveless vest revealed thick-muscled arms that hung loose but ready. On his upper arm, a harp embla-zoned with shamrocks was tattooed in emerald green. His grip, when it came, was friendly and firm, but his pinched eyes made obscure calculations. In the hallway behind McCabe, Robby saw Eamon's rifle propped up against the stair-rails.

'Shame you never met him,' McCabe added, in his broad border-county guttural. 'We were great mates, so we were. Weren't we, Eamon? Me and Sean, hah?'

'That's right,' Eamon agreed, furtive in his fireside crouch. 'We were all great mates.'

Robby shuffled uneasily. McCabe didn't ease the pres-sure on his hand, though it wasn't the deliberate show of strength Robby had first thought it might be. Their un-welcome guest's mind was elsewhere.

'Except for O'Neill. I'll do away with him yet,' he mused. 'Himself and his soft Donegal accent, hah? Didn't he sound the dead spit of Packie Bonner, Eamon?'

'Now that you mention it, he did and all. Only O'Neill was never good for anything.'

'I never liked Packie Bonner either,' McCabe said, his hold on Robby tightening. 'He let in a right soft goal against Italy in 1990. We coulda won the World Cup that time, only for him. I watched that match in prison. Won't be watching any more World Cups in there. Isn't that right, Eamon, hah?'

'They'll have to get up early in the morning to catch you, Razor,' Eamon said.

Putting his arm over Robby's shoulder, McCabe brought him to where Eamon sat. Robby didn't know which was worse, the stink of McCabe's unwashed armpit or the stench from his mouth.

'You didn't answer Eamon's question yet, Robby.'

Eamon and Robby stared at each other, nonplussed.

'I think Eamon was a bit worried about you. About where you were and it so late.'

'I was in town. At the pictures.'

The poker rasped dully along the grate as Eamon raked the ashes, trying to ignore what was happening.

'With your mates, I suppose? Bet you have loads of mates, being the son of a hero and all, hah?'

'Yeah,' Robby answered. 'We went for chips after. I wasn't watching the time.'

'Go 'way out of that. You were with a young one, I bet.'

McCabe released him with a nudge and a knowing wink. Disgusted, Robby went to the cooker, got the kettle and filled it noisily.

Any urge to show his contempt evaporated as he wondered about the New Agers. Had McCabe seen them? Had he seen Robby at the stone circle with them?

'Touched a nerve there, Robby, didn't I?' McCabe laughed. 'A fine big lad like you, bet you have to beat the young ones away with a stick.'

There was a manic, forced quality to his joviality, and his darting eyes seemed intent on provocation.

Robby held up the filled kettle.

'Would you like some tea? And something to eat?'

'You're a mind-reader, Robby boy. He's a wee mind-reader, Eamon, isn't he? You wouldn't get away with much and that lad around, I bet.'

'He's a good lad. His father would be proud of him.' Eamon's smile was a pathetic apology. Robby turned to the cooker, unimpressed. He took some rashers and sausages from the fridge and put them in a frying-pan caked with the sooty grease of too many meals.

The heat from the cooker soon made a furnace of the kitchen. McCabe, deep in hushed conversation with Eamon, reacted sharply to every clang of pot and pan. Sweating, agitated, his face snapped towards Robby each time, and each time there was a momentary delay before his smile returned.

'Don't mind me, Robby. I'm a bit nervy,' McCabe said. 'That's a grand smell there. Good man.'

'It's all ready now. Do you want to sit up?'

'By God, you're well served here, Eamon. Bet you don't have to lift a finger.'

'He's a great worker,' Eamon said dismally. 'He does everything.'

'The old leg still as bad as ever, is it?' McCabe asked as he took a seat at the table.

Eamon nodded, apparently unaware of the sarcasm in McCabe's enquiry. He placed the poker against the surround of the fireplace and lifted himself from his armchair.

'I'll go and fix up the cellar for you, Razor. It's not too comfortable, mind, but sure ... sure you'll be moving on soon, I suppose.'

McCabe picked up a sausage from the plate with his fingers, chewed it down to a stump and then swallowed the stump.

'You needn't go fixing up anything at all, Eamon.'

Eamon's face was suddenly bright with relief. 'Are you not staying?' he asked.

They waited while another sausage suffered the same fate as the first. McCabe wiped his fingers on his vest.

'That's mighty stuff, Robby. Mighty.'

He kept them waiting while he demolished the last of the sausages, his lips glistening with grease.

'You're not away now?' Eamon said, his laugh strained and dry. 'Sure you'll have to rest before you go.'

McCabe held out his cup for a refill and eyed Eamon as the tea was poured.

'Oh, I'll be resting here all right, Eamon. But not in any cellar. I spent eight years in solitary. That's enough of cellars for any man. No, this is a fine big house and there's plenty of sheds out there. I'll move around. I like to move around, even when I'm resting.'

Eamon felt behind him for the refuge of his chair. His arms shook under his weight as he lowered himself down. Distracted, Robby filled McCabe's cup to the very brim. McCabe stared at the spilling tea disinterestedly. He flicked the cup sideways and let the overflow splash out on to the oilcloth table-cover. He considered the spreading puddle.

'When I was a little lad — I'd have been, what, about five or six — I went to sleep one Christmas Eve with one eye open to see Santa Claus. Not that the bastard ever left us very much. Never lost the habit, though. See, you never know what kind of surprise might be in store for you. You never know who the hell might be dressed up as Santa Claus, hah?'

chapter *12*

When Robby woke, he knew it was after midday, because the sun had moved from the front to the back of the house. He hadn't fallen asleep until dawn had begun to pencil in the outline of hills on the horizon. It had been a night filled with imaginary conversations, and in all of them he had been the leper ringing his warning bell and calling 'Keep away from me! Stay away from Cloghercree!'

The midnight meeting with the New Agers at the stones was just a dream now; the pleasant expectation of going to their camp and seeing what their lives were like, seeing Mayfly and that woman again, had been reduced to wishful thinking. He'd have to play Action Man and warn them off, for their own good.

And O'Neill? There was only one way to ensure that he stayed away. It wouldn't be easy to go to their house, apologise for what he'd said to Grace, and pretend there were no hard feelings, but what choice did Robby have?

The conversations playing themselves out in his mind never ended well, no matter how hard he tried. As he struggled wearily out of bed, he didn't believe the real thing would be any better — if he ever got to leave the house in the first place. That was another conversation that held little promise: asking McCabe if he could go out, like a sickly schoolboy pleading with a fearsome teacher.

The chill of McCabe's presence made the house feel colder than ever. The doors of the three spare bedrooms, always locked, stood open, casting more light on the landing than the old house could bear. A murky wash of yellow, brown and grey covered walls and ceilings whose cracked plaster was an indecipherable map of endless tributaries. In one high corner, a mushroom sprouted among the ragged, sooty cobwebs.

The bare boards of the staircase creaked beneath Robby's feet. At the far end of the hallway, behind the stairs, five granite steps led to the cellar door, which was wide open, exposing the junk that was piled high. Broken furniture; old paint tins; Eamon's traps; a big old cabinet radio with its glass face smashed in ... the debris of four generations.

Pausing by the kitchen door, Robby listened for a moment, heard only his great-uncle's familiar pottering, and went inside. Eamon knelt at the fireplace, filling an iron bucket with ashes. The hand holding the shovel shook, and when Robby spoke, the ashes tumbled and rose in a sandstorm cloud.

'Where is he?' Robby asked.

Eamon dropped the shovel into the bucket, sending up another grainy gust. 'Will you keep it down, he could be anywhere. I haven't seen a sign of him since we came back from the cemetery.'

'You brought him to the cemetery? Are you crazy? You could've been seen with him.'

'No one ever goes down there,' Eamon said sourly. 'Not at that time of the morning.'

Robby knew he had no right to be offended, but the thought of McCabe sneaking around his father's grave was unbearable.

'You said he wouldn't come,' he said. 'You were lying. You knew all along.'

Still on his knees among the ashes, Eamon rubbed his bleary eyes with a dusty hand. 'I didn't, Robby, I swear.' The denial rang hollow. 'He won't stay long, but while he's here, don't cross him, Robby. A couple of days, at most, and he'll be gone.'

'Yeah, right. Where, Eamon, where the hell is he going to go?'

'There's plenty of safe houses.'

'Not for him, there aren't. You know that as well I do.'

'He'll find a way out. He always did,' Eamon insisted. 'Don't make an enemy of him, Robby. He's OK to his friends — believe me, I know. But ....'

'But what? But he takes a razor to his enemies?'

Robby went about making himself some breakfast and washing up the previous day's mess. If McCabe did let him go out, he thought, what was to stop him walking into the garda station, or even walking away for good? Nothing, except the fact that Eamon would be a sitting target for revenge. Robby despised his great-uncle, but not that much. He didn't think he ever could.

'They must have a dog below on the back road, those knackers,' Eamon said. Robby ignored him, scrubbing hard at the submerged plates.

'I woke up around six with all the howling,' Eamon continued. 'I'll have to go down and see them off. Can't be putting up with that carry-on.'

'I'll go,' Robby told him.

A shadow fell across him from the doorway.

'There's no need to do that, Robby,' McCabe said. He was holding Eamon's rifle casually in one hand. He looked like he'd slept no better than Eamon or Robby. He needed a shave again, and his clothes were festooned with straw.

He sat down at the table, setting the rifle on his lap. 'Is there tea in it?'

Robby placed a clean cup before him and poured.

'A drop of ....' McCabe began, but Robby was already reaching for the milk carton. 'Mind-reading again, hah? Bet you're always a step ahead of the posse.'

The sound of Eamon nervously clearing his throat

drew McCabe's attention away from Robby. He wasn't pleased with the interruption.

'We can't have those knackers hanging around,' Eamon said. 'They'll draw the guards on us.'

'Was there anything on the news about me?' McCabe asked, gruffly dismissing Eamon's concern.

'I didn't see the news, Razor. But I'm telling you, those knackers ....'

McCabe set his cup on the table too sharply and the tea splashed over his fingers. He grimaced at the pain.

'You're telling me, you're telling me,' he repeated. Then, reining in his anger, he licked the brown liquid from his hand. 'On the radio, so. Was there anything on the radio?' He surveyed the kitchen like a great black crow scanning a field for worms. 'Where *is* the radio?'

'It's broken.' Eamon shrugged. 'We only have the telly. There's news at one o'clock.'

'And what time is it now?'

'We can't wear watches. They just stop for some reason,' Eamon said. 'But it's nearly one now ... I think.'

'And the grandfather clock on the landing has only one hand.' McCabe shook his head and looked disdainfully from one of them to the other. 'No wonder ye stay in bed half the day.'

Robby leaned over from the sink and switched on the TV. Even as he turned the volume up to Eamon's pitch, he knew he was acting rashly. For some reason he thought of his father. Maybe Sean was a hero after all; to be a hero you had to be dumb or crazy or both. Maybe dumbness and craziness were in the Wade genes.

As if to confirm his own theory, he said, 'We don't always get up so late.'

'What did you say?' McCabe shouted above the theme music of a soap opera. 'Turn that bloody thing down.'

'I'm a bit hard of hearing, Razor,' Eamon said.

'Turn it down, Robby,' McCabe repeated. 'What did you just say to me?'

Behind him, Eamon hobbled towards the door to the farmyard. 'I'll go down to them knackers while you're watching the news,' he said.

'Stay where you are, Eamon,' McCabe ordered. 'Robby?'

'I said ....' Robby swallowed the bile in his throat. 'I said, we don't always get up so late. We had a bad night, with the dog barking and all. It must have kept you awake too.'

While McCabe considered Robby's answer, Eamon began to limp towards the door again.

'Eamon?' McCabe said quietly. 'Did I ask you to stay put, did I?'

'But the knackers —'

'They're a harmless bunch of weirdos. All peace and love and all that crap. The way I see it, if the guards see these hippies hanging around, they won't suspect I'm here. They'll think it'd be too risky for me to stay here with that lot about. Reverse psychology, they call it, Eamon. You have to figure out what they're thinking, what they think you're thinking. Know what I mean? These knackers are just the cover I need. The longer they stay put, the better for me, I reckon.'

Robby sat down at the table. He poured himself some tea, careful not to allow even a hint of a tremor in his hand.

'Is anyone else likely to be coming up here?' McCabe asked him. 'Your mother? Or O'Neill?'

'They don't call,' Robby said. 'I go into town to see Mam. I was supposed to go today.'

Eamon looked across at him, open-mouthed and uncomprehending.

'We'll see about that,' McCabe answered. 'Anyone else?'

'No. Unless Tommy the Tramp comes. He sleeps in the car sometimes, out in the garage. He's harmless.'

'Razor,' Eamon pleaded, 'the guards were here twice yesterday. They're sure to —'

'Three times,' McCabe corrected him. 'They only came to the front gate, the third time. You wouldn't have seen them from the house.'

Robby was glad he'd finished filling his cup. If McCabe knew the guards had been there, then he'd been hovering around the farm all day.

The smile returned to McCabe's face.

'Eamon was telling me you had to shoot your dog yesterday,' he said. 'Shame about that.'

'Why did you stay when you knew the guards were hassling us, Razor?' Eamon asked. 'You know they won't let up.'

'Because if they really thought I was here, do you think they'd be driving out in their squad cars and uniforms, hah? Wouldn't you say they'd be more likely to come sneaking around in unmarked cars, armed for a gunfight? They're stupid, Eamon, but they're not that stupid.'

On the TV, the news bulletin began. McCabe sat in Eamon's armchair, while Eamon pulled over a chair from the table. Robby stayed at the table, feeling strangely detached from the two men and from the newscaster's urgency.

'Time you got that yoke fixed, Eamon,' McCabe muttered. The announcer gave details of the kidnap victim's and the injured guard's conditions. Showing no trace of emotion, McCabe absorbed the news of a supposed sighting of him in County Clare, eighty miles from Cloghercree, and repeated warnings not to approach this 'dangerously unstable character'. Robby sipped at his tea, but it had gone cold.

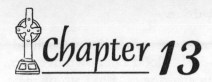 **chapter 13**

Mayfly's night had been as long and sleepless as Robby's. There were times when Rusty's howls and fitful spasms had her crouching with her eyes jammed tight shut and her fists pressed to her ears. Three, four times, she tried to pick him up, with the mad intention of going up to the house in spite of the late hour. Rusty snarled at her, baring teeth coated green by the herbal mixture. Retreating, Mayfly was at once frightened of him and frightened for him. He thrashed about, his red-veined eyes rounding on her with malice.

The birds in the grove behind the cottage had settled into their singing day when Rusty's delirium subsided abruptly. Mayfly waited for a last shivering heave, a croaking final bark. Instead, she saw the crumpled blanket begin to rise and fall in an easy rhythm. With no great hope that this was anything more than a brief respite, she tried for a snatch of wary sleep.

Wild dogs roamed the Stone Field in her dreams, guarding the standing stones that were skyscraper-high. Though she had no idea why, she knew she had to get inside the towering circle. She stood before the largest and most vicious of the rabid hounds, out-staring it until she floated past, her feet seeming to glide along the very tips of the grass-blades below.

A vast brightness flowed from the entrance to the stone circle. Mayfly saw her mother sitting inside. Andy's familiar white dress glowed and was gently buffeted by a breeze Mayfly couldn't feel. Her expression was unfettered by care or pain as she beckoned Mayfly inward.

All at once, Mayfly's arm was gripped from behind. Sharp teeth sank into her flesh. Blood ran down her arm. She tried to break free, but the dog was too strong. The stone circle began to recede. Andy waved, and the distance became too great for Mayfly to see whether she was still smiling or if she cried for her departing daughter. 'Andy!' Mayfly called, her own voice as far away as her mother's fading image. 'Andy!'

'Fly, it's OK, you've been dreaming,' Bubble said, as her eyes filled up with the sunlight streaming in through the open cottage door. 'I've come up here a couple of times to check you out.'

'Why?' Mayfly asked, withdrawing from the hand on her arm. 'What's wrong?'

'Nothing. But you're always such an early bird, and it's after one now.' On the floor beside her he'd placed a cup of peppermint tea and some buttered soda bread. 'Got the bread in town this morning. Home-made; just wait until you taste it. Terrific stuff.'

Rusty lay in the centre of the flagstoned floor, his blanket tossed to one side. His breath came slowly, hardly raising his pink underbelly. Bubble knelt and replaced the blanket, careful not to disturb the unconscious dog.

'A red setter,' he said. 'Beautiful dogs, setters. We always had them when I was a kid. Pity Andy didn't ....'

Still emerging from her dream, Mayfly was slightly baffled by what he was saying. She'd understood that Bubble and Andy were as one in their aversion to dogs.

'He's had a bad night,' Bubble said.

Mayfly sipped the lukewarm tea and ate the bread, though she had no appetite. There was nothing special about the taste. Home-made or not, the bread went down in doughy lumps and the butter had a raw, salty edge to it. Her back and neck ached. The sunlight, spreading across her legs, made her shiver.

'I had a bad night too,' she said.

'We all had, Fly.' Bubble glanced uneasily about the floor, as though he'd lost something and might find it there.

'Andy? Is she all right?'

'Andy's fine,' he said. 'Andy's so perfect, so *well*, it scares me, Mayfly.'

He was looking at her, and she saw that he wasn't exaggerating. The lines on his craggy face had never seemed so furrowed, nor the blue eyes so awash with trepidation.

'She's had a good rest,' Mayfly said. 'It's only natural for her to feel a little better.'

Her throat felt dry, and for a moment that was terrifyingly long, she imagined she'd forgotten how to swallow.

'This is different. It feels like ....' Surprising himself with a sudden insight, Bubble raised himself from his kneeling position beside Rusty. 'You know what it feels like?' He gazed at his daughter with blind intensity. 'Like when she was expecting you. After she got past the morning sickness and all that. She was, like, charged with life. Fly, you could feel the air around her crackle. You can feel the same thing now.'

'Andy's making the best of things, like she always does. For your sake.'

'For our sake,' Bubble answered. 'No, this is ... I was going to say "the real thing", but how can it be real, man? Remember that Steve Martin film we went to see a few years back — the one about this faith healer guy, faking miracles until one day he performs a real miracle and he can't deal with it? That's how I feel.'

If Andy was pretending to be well, Mayfly thought, she'd gone a kindness too far. She felt a sneaking sympathy for Bubble. Then again, she would have pitied anyone who could be fooled so easily.

'First thing this morning, she's up making breakfast ....'

'You let her do that!'

'I had no choice. I was still asleep,' Bubble explained. 'Then she announces we're going into town. Comes up here with your tea and porridge, to see if you wanted to come, but she didn't want to wake you. So in we go. And she buys this new dress — well, something from one of those second-hand places — and a big, floppy straw hat like she used to wear, way back when. I was racing after her, man, telling her to slow down. But she tells me she can't go any slower.'

She buys this new dress. Andy never bought anything without asking Mayfly's opinion first. In fact, Andy never bought anything for herself unless Mayfly was there to absolutely insist.

'Fly?' Bubble asked. 'Will you come on up to Nirvana and tell me I'm not wrong about this? See what *you* think?'

Mayfly almost wished things had remained as they were: Andy continuing to decline, slowly, inevitably, and new dresses the last thing on her mind.

'I'm tired, Bubble,' she said, avoiding the suddenly appalled look on his face. 'I'll follow you up later.'

Bubble crossed the floor, his feet crunching on the debris of broken, reduced things. At the doorway, he paused.

'She's waiting up there to show you her new gear, Fly. You're going to deny her that, are you? You don't think she deserves to spend a few measly pounds on herself for a change? All her life, Andy's had nothing that someone else hadn't already worn or used, and —'

'And whose fault is that? You had everything, every chance. You couldn't give Andy a decent life. You threw it all away to live out some dumb escapist fantasy.'

Mayfly couldn't see his reaction. He was slouching, his back to the light, in the bright doorway.

'Chances, yeah, chances. Paid for with my father's blood money,' he said.

'Spare me the old Sir Gordon lecture, will you? Rich

equals bad, poor equals good and all that. It doesn't add up any more.'

'No, but maybe it's time I told you the whole story. I should've done, long ago. Sometimes I forget how quickly you're growing up. How quickly you've had to grow up.'

'I don't want to hear any more of your excuses.'

All the while, the image of her parents wandering happily around town, without her, refused to be budged.

'Hear me out, Mayfly. See if you think it's an excuse. Maybe it is.'

She reached down and spread her hands out on the floor, as though she might keel over at any moment. One palm felt the sting of heat from the sun-baked flagstone; the other, in shadow, felt the chill that was the stone's natural state.

'We were discouraged from asking about Dad's work,' Bubble said. 'Top secret, we were told, and when I was a kid that was all right. I mean, I actually fancied he was some kind of James Bond type. In any case, I saw very little of him. Or of Mother. She had her horses and her busy social life. I was fourteen, maybe fifteen, before it really got to me. I began to act the rebel. It happens, even at Eton. Dad hated socialism, communism, so I decided all that lefty stuff was for me.'

Incredibly, Rusty was beginning to crawl towards Mayfly, panting softly as if to urge himself on. Bubble gazed out at the green glorious day.

'Every month I'd get this magazine — Spotlight, I think it was called. Lots of stuff about how the major powers were arming right-wing dictatorships in South America and Africa and south-east Asia. Anyway, to cut a long story short, I found Sir Gordon's name there. His company was supplying arms to the apartheid régime. Well, I freaked out. I'd just turned seventeen. Mother, of course, didn't want to talk about it, and Dad lectured me on his contribution

to world stability — and on my ingratitude for the privi-
leges I'd been given.'

Rusty clawed his way across the floor. The sound of
his nails on the stone was like grit scraping Mayfly's teeth.

'I had a friend at Eton — chap called Anthony. His
parents lived in America. I told Mother I'd been invited
over for Easter, and she approved because Anthony's
people were "well connected". I left and I never went
back. They found me in California when I was nineteen.
Or, rather, the private investigator they hired found me.
But they never came, and they never asked me to come
back. Not that I would have, but it might have meant
something if they had.'

Bubble was less the man of great principle now, more
the abandoned little boy. Rusty made one final effort and
his head, heavy with fatigue, rolled onto Mayfly's lap. She
stroked the wispy down on his forehead. There was no
joy in the realisation that he was going to live. He had
been hers only when he was ill and dying. Now that he
was well, he'd have to go back where he really belonged.

'You know, it would make my parents very happy,'
Bubble continued, 'if you went and told them I'd failed
you. They always liked to be proved right.'

He moved forward, and Mayfly could see his face
again. His expression betrayed neither anger nor sorrow.

'I'm deadly serious. Maybe you should go to them.'

'Oh, shut up, Bubble. Leave me alone.'

No desperate return to Rainbow Shades could colour
the grey void in her mind. Grey. Ash, lead, the hospital-
grey of Andy's face after the second futile operation.

'What about Andy? Please come, Mayfly, come with
me now.'

Grey, the worst, the ugliest, the filthy mix of every
rainbow shade flung together in an ugly murk. Grey. You
couldn't play games with grey.

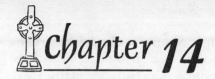

chapter 14

Robby stood at the gate of the Stone Field and watched the smoke from the far-off campfire billow upwards. The evening sky, salmon-pink in the distance, held only a few puffballs of cloud. He was an hour late, having spent the evening considering whether he should go at all. The day's portents hadn't been good.

'Ye can come and go as ye please, either of ye. People might only be asking questions if they don't see ye around. Just as long as one of ye stays here with me. At all times,' McCabe had said. The threat was clear. Whenever Robby chose to leave the house, Eamon became a hostage.

If Eamon was aware of his friend's barely-disguised malevolence, he wasn't letting on. Instead, he'd tried pathetically to lighten the atmosphere.

'Great to be young, all the same, Razor. Always on the go, Robby is.'

'Must be taking after his father, so,' was McCabe's pointed answer.

CB

O'Neill's car hadn't been in the driveway when Robby got to the house, in mid-afternoon. His relief, however, was short-lived. Long after he realised Grace had probably gone to the garage office, he kept ringing the doorbell. There was something forlorn about that sound, echoing in the empty hallway inside, that made him want to hear it over and over again. It was like a song that broke your heart so badly, you didn't want to listen to anything else for hours on end. Like Jeff Buckley singing 'Hallelujah'.

Eventually he went around the house, through a timber

arch twined with flowering clematis, to the back garden. Perfectly trimmed grass, not a weed in sight; neat rockeries; a little artificial pond with a miniature fountain. He'd buy them a freaky little plastic leprechaun for Christmas. Bet they'd like that.

Beyond his reflection in the long patio doors, he saw the tidy clutter of the life that Grace and O'Neill had made for themselves — a life their child would soon share. Two colourful coffee mugs, with matching coasters, on the long pine table; a glossy magazine left open on a wicker chair; a pair of newly polished football boots arranged neatly on a sheet of newspaper, drying in the sun. For no reason he could think of, Robby tried the handle. The door was locked.

'What are you up to?' At first, he almost thought the voice was in his head. Then he heard an urgent rustling in the hedge at the end of the garden. An elderly man, his wispy white hair tossed from his gardening exertions, peered myopically through thick spectacles. 'Get out of there or I'll call the guards!'

Robby could hardly be surprised at not being recognised as Grace's son, his visits were so infrequent. But, stirred so abruptly from such a depth of sadness, he exploded in anger. He picked up a fistful of fancy pebbles from between some miniature shrubs and let fly. From behind the hedge came a yelp and an impassioned call of 'Maisie! Maisie, ring the guards! There's a robber in O'Neill's back garden!'

Making good his escape, Robby kicked out at the trellised arch at the side of the house. To his horror, the thing collapsed around him. He thought about trying to fix it, but if this Maisie character really had rung the guards, they'd be on their way already.

When Robby reached the garage, five sweating minutes later, his luck didn't improve.

There had been a time when he had relished the hours spent in the narrow, high-ceilinged shed that had room for four cars at a squeeze. Under the bonnets of Fords, Toyotas, Volkswagens, Citroëns, he'd followed O'Neill's explanations and passed the three-quarter-inch spanner or the Phillips screwdriver. Back then, he'd imagined no other life than that of a garage mechanic, and no more exciting prospect — apart from dying 'for Ireland only', of course — than one day driving his own car out of that garage. Now, the very smell of motor oil made him gag. It was the scent of betrayal.

Grace and O'Neill had gone to Galway city and were staying overnight. The news was delivered by Eddie Dunphy, one of the mechanics. Eddie was a hulking, middle-aged biker with hair tumbling greasily down his back to make up for the bald spot on top.

'Something about a check-up at that private hospital. Nothing but the best for Grace,' he added. He made a cigarette appear from behind his ear and lit up, oblivious of the No Smoking sign above his head and the pools of oil under his feet.

'Is she all right?' Robby paled, remembering the scene with Grace at Cloghercree.

'No sweat, Robby,' Eddie said laconically. 'The women are always going for check-ups when they're pregnant. I should know. Four little headbangers at home. Telling you, man, we were up and down the road to Ballinasloe Hospital on the bike, non-stop.'

'You brought your missus for check-ups — on the motorbike?'

'Yeah.' The mechanic remained unfazed. 'She was wearing a helmet, like.'

Talking to Eddie, always so daft and laid-back, cheered Robby up — until he became bothered again at how Grace's life was going on without him. What did he expect, after he'd avoided her for months on end and then spoken to her as he had? He cut short Eddie's delighted description of his latest biker outing to Wexford and asked him to tell Grace he'd call in to see her the next evening.

As Robby slouched away from the garage, Eddie called after him, 'You want to make up your mind about the job here. There's lads queueing up to get in here, and no sign of Liam taking anyone on. Says he's waiting for you to decide.'

'I don't think so, Eddie.'

'Scout's honour, Robby,' Eddie said. 'Couldn't find a better guy to work for. Liam's sound — for a head honcho, like.'

'I've already decided,' Robby answered sourly. 'I wouldn't work in this kip for a thousand a week.'

☙

Now, six hours later, Robby had left Eamon to play the hostage again. As he climbed the Stone Field gate, McCabe's playful menace was still in his thoughts.

'You won't be too long, sure you won't, hah?'

'No.'

'What's her name, Robby?'

'I don't have a girlfriend.'

'Come on, Robby, you're among friends. Tell us, come on, don't be shy.' McCabe's smile was wide, but his eyes held a deadly seriousness. 'Sure, we can't let him off if we don't know if she's suitable. Isn't that right, Eamon? We don't want Robby dragging around after some tramp of a young one, do we, hah?'

Eamon couldn't get his head any lower than it already was. The best he could do was hide his face behind his hand.

McCabe was waiting, and it wasn't a game any more. He was striking a bargain. Robby could go if he told him the girl's name.

He was about to invent one when he realised it mightn't be beyond McCabe to find a way of checking the name out. He remembered a former classmate, a girl he'd liked but who'd had no time for the son of an IRA martyr.

'Mary Dooley,' Robby said. 'She lives in Blackcastle Avenue.'

'See!' McCabe exclaimed. 'I was right, Eamon. You'd better hurry, Robby, you don't want to keep Mary waiting.'

At the stone circle, Robby looked back towards the gate. The path — invisible now — from the gate to the cottage had never been a straight one; it had always meandered like a river. But now, looking back at the curving line of trodden grass where he had walked, he was thinking, not of rivers, but of slithering, reptilian things.

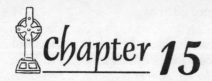

chapter 15

There was no doubting the transformation in Andy. Her bandage was in place beneath the broad-brimmed straw hat, and her lips were as worryingly bloodless as before; but the vitality Bubble had spoken of was unmistakably present in her every movement. And yet Mayfly was unrelentingly wary. All evening, as she helped her mother prepare the meal, she refused to look at the stone circle, as a superstitious child avoids the cracks in a pavement.

To Mayfly, cooking was always a chore, perhaps because whatever she cooked never seemed to taste as good as her mother's efforts. Andy, on the other hand, went about the task with enthusiasm, that evening more than ever. Nothing was too much trouble — stuffed red peppers, creamed cauliflower with white sauce, sesame-seed-and-honey biscuits ....

As they sat around the campfire, Mayfly wondered if Andy was a little disappointed by the muted atmosphere that surrounded their feast.

The guest of honour's sullenness bordered on ingratitude. Mayfly might have been angry at Robby, had she herself not been so subdued and so afraid to believe her eyes. Bubble was afraid too, but his fear expressed itself differently — in nervous chuckling, bursts of laughter when he dropped his fork or poured too much sea salt onto his cauliflower or dished out the compliments to Andy too fulsomely. Mayfly suspected that he'd been hiding his doubts in one sneaked joint too many.

'Incredible, man. I'd forgotten food could taste so good, Andy.'

Mayfly didn't take offence. She was more concerned that his boyish nervousness would end badly. She'd seen him like this before — when Andy had come out of hospital after her operation. Usually so reserved and self-contained, he'd spoken without thinking, speaking because he felt he had to fill the silences and, in his anxiety, saying the stupidest things.

When Bubble did finally put his foot in it, Mayfly was surprised to find she was glad he had.

'Must be cool to live so close to nature, Robby,' he enthused. 'You know, have your own piece of the earth, work it. It's how we were meant to live, man.'

'My great-uncle owns the place. He doesn't do much, apart from keeping a few cattle.'

'He doesn't grow stuff? Wheat, oats, vegetables?'

'Grass,' Robby said flatly.

'Man, if I had a couple of fields, I'd grow organic veg. You know how hard it is to get that stuff in the shops?'

'My great-uncle likes an easy life.'

'You living with him or just staying over?' Exactly the question he shouldn't have asked, Mayfly guessed from Robby's downcast face, but precisely what she'd wanted him to ask.

'My father's dead. Mam lives in town. She got married. Yeah, I live here.'

When Robby spoke, which he had only very occasionally over the past half-hour, it was in brief, self-conscious snatches. He was like someone who'd lost the art of conversation. Mayfly couldn't recall ever encountering such solitariness in a person.

'Let me take your plate, Robby,' Andy said, seeming to glide into the space between Bubble and Robby so that each was spared the embarrassment of the other. 'Would you like to try some of my muesli cookies? And, hey, don't feel you have to. I won't fall apart if you don't, right?'

'No,' Robby answered. 'I mean, yes, I will. Try them ... have some.'

'Bubble, why don't you get the guitar while I pour the tea,' Andy suggested. 'Nettle tea, Robby, that OK with you?'

'Nettle? Yeah, sounds ... good.'

'It's getting late,' Bubble said, having tried for a nod of approval from Mayfly and got none. 'And we haven't told Robby about the stones yet.'

'You tell him,' Andy said. 'I'll go get the guitar.'

'People come all the time.' Robby's discomfort had him shifting about for a more comfortable way to sit. 'There's no need to explain.'

Mayfly hoped that Bubble would leave it at that, but she didn't really expect he would. Too fired up with optimism, too deflated by doubt, he hung in a precarious balance, desperate to be rescued by some reassurance. Though they pretended not to, he and Mayfly watched Andy's progress towards Nirvana — a progress that was noticeably more hesitant than it had been only a few hours earlier.

'We came to find a cure,' Bubble said, in an anguished voice that threatened to break Mayfly's façade of indifference. 'My wife is very ill — she's .... Have you heard of people being cured at the stones, Robby? Old legends, that kind of thing?'

For all the effort that went into it, Robby's answer was unconvincing.

'Yeah, I've heard stories. My great-uncle's told me stuff that happened there. A long time ago, like. People don't come for cures now, but they used to, back in the last century and back in the old days. I mean, the older days, the Middle Ages ....'

None of it rang true, but somehow it confirmed that Robby had a heart. He didn't want to disappoint Bubble, who hung on his every word.

'Really?' Bubble exclaimed.

When Mayfly caught Robby's eye, she knew that on the question of miracles, at least, they understood each other.

The zing of guitar strings brushing against Andy's new blue dress reached Mayfly's ears. She wanted to hear music. Even Bubble's.

'What kind of music do you like, Robby?' she asked, surprising herself and surprising him even more.

'Oasis ....' Robby faltered. 'Gomez ... Jeff Buckley ....'

'Tim's son. Couldn't believe it when he died so young, just like his father,' Bubble mused. 'I played on Tim's last album. Weird how their stuff is so connected. I mean, the kid was so young when Tim died, maybe didn't even listen to his father's stuff when he was growing up. But it's like they were on the same journey, man. Like no matter where Jeff walked, he found himself on the same road his father walked. Further along, maybe, but the same road.'

This time, Robby was unable to disguise his amazed disbelief.

Andy had returned, bristling with energy again. She handed the guitar to Bubble.

'It's true,' she told Robby. 'Bubble gigged with the best of them.'

'That's me,' Bubble said. 'Played on everyone else's albums, never had one of my own. Robby doesn't want to hear an old dog howling at the moon.'

But Robby clearly did. Bubble was a damned fool, but when he sang, he was such a sweet one that Mayfly understood how her mother had followed him down all those roads that had turned out to be cul-de-sacs.

Andy was still travelling with him, retracing their steps, punctuating each song with stories of their wanderings.

To India in 1976 — 'hell on wheels,' Andy proclaimed

— in search of a maharishi who, when they got there, had
packed up and gone to the California they'd just left.
Anti-nuclear gatherings in France, England, Wales. Sun
festivals in Spain, moon festivals in Sweden. Andy remembered the places but had to look to Bubble to confirm
the years.

The songs went from a few, to a dozen, to twenty and
more — Tim Buckley, Bob Dylan, James Taylor, Leonard
Cohen, more Bob Dylan .... Somewhere in the middle of
all this, Bubble rolled a joint and he and Andy passed it
back and forth. To Mayfly's relief, he didn't offer it to
Robby, who, in any case, seemed oblivious to anything but
the music. His bashfulness had melted away to such an
extent that he was tentatively joining in on 'To Ramona'
and 'The Times They Are A-Changing'.

Quite why her mood plunged to even greater depths
than before, Mayfly wasn't sure. Too many sad, slow
songs, perhaps; or the moments of exasperated confusion
in Andy's recollections — 'No, not St Louis. New Orleans,
was it?'; or the unexpected smallness of Robby's singing
voice.

Another song ended, and she found herself standing
above the others as the flames of the campfire receded.

'I'm going to check on Rusty,' she said. 'Then I'm going
to bed. I'm whacked.'

'What about the stones?' Bubble asked.

'Fly's tired,' Andy said. 'We'll go.'

Bubble shook his head and set the guitar aside.

Robby stood up and brushed the straw and white fire-
ash off his combats.

'Time I got home,' he said. 'Thanks for everything.'

'Come again, Robby, won't you?' Andy asked. 'We enjoyed your company. Didn't we, Bubble?'

'Yeah, we sure did. Hope I didn't bore your socks off,
man. I'll see if I can lay my hands on that album for you.

The one I did with Tim Buckley. Good title — appropriate, you know. *Look at the Fool.*'

Already walking away, Mayfly glanced back over her shoulder. Robby was standing like a stranger lost at a crossroads, unable to read the signposts. Then she saw Andy look up at him and nod as if in assent.

She was by the dormobile when he caught up with her.

'Could I see Rusty before I go?' he asked.

'He's your dog.'

They went along the back road together.

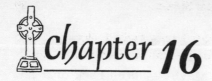

chapter 16

Robby's tense alertness to the night noises around them irritated Mayfly. Every secretive flurry in the hedgerow, every swift rustle in the fields, drew his sharp attention. When she stopped at the cottage gate, he asked in a strangled whisper, 'You're keeping Rusty here?'

'Is that a problem?'

'No, I suppose not,' he stammered. 'Rusty loves the cottage. We used to live here when I was young.'

'Really? Well, we've got something in common, then. I'm living here now. For a few days, anyway.'

She was having trouble with the clasp of the gate and he reached across her to open it with familiar ease. He was standing very close to her and they were both momentarily lost for words. His breath on her hair was a warm breeze that made her shiveringly aware of the night's cold.

'Who owns the cottage now?' Mayfly asked. When she looked up into Robby's eyes, the collar of her denim jacket set the hairs on the back of her neck tingling.

Robby answered reluctantly, retreating a step or two and staring at the moon-white walls.

'Eamon. My great-uncle.'

'Does he give you a hard time?'

'He's old,' Robby said. 'He's not very happy with how his life went. He takes it out on everyone else.'

'Will he take it out on me for staying here?'

Robby shrugged, started to say something but changed his mind. Mayfly went determinedly along the short path to the cottage door. She had no right to this place, but neither had Robby's great-uncle any right to let it lie idle and fall into such disrepair. He couldn't abandon something and still call it his.

'I'll only be here for a couple of nights,' she said.

Rusty's wheezy excitement on seeing Robby at the door was a welcome diversion, at first. It felt good to have made such a moment possible, to have succeeded even once in putting right something that had gone cruelly, unfairly wrong.

'I can't believe this,' Robby said in surprise and delight, nuzzling Rusty, who slavered ecstatically in his lap. 'You're a miracle-worker.'

'It was Andy. She told me what to do.'

Mayfly switched on the torch on the mantelpiece so that he could see the dog more clearly.

'We don't need the light, do we?' he said urgently. 'We can pull back those curtains. It's a bright night.'

Her irritation growing, she flicked the switch again and plunged them into darkness. Edging across to where she guessed the window to be, she brushed against Robby and felt the muscles of his back tense up.

'Sorry,' he muttered. When she swept back the makeshift curtains, she saw that his pleasure at finding Rusty alive and well had already diminished.

'Maybe you should take him home with you, now he's on the mend.'

'No. Eamon would have a bloody heart attack if I brought him back tonight. I'll have to break it to him gently, you know.'

'Won't he be pleased to have Rusty back?'

'Not particularly.'

Mayfly sat down on her sleeping-bag, which lay beside Rusty's blanket. Robby adjusted Rusty's weight in his lap, moving further away from her as he did so.

'I didn't want to shoot him,' he said, gently brushing

the fur on Rusty's back. 'Eamon told me the vet was sure he was finished. I didn't want him to die in some surgery. The grove out there, that's his favourite place. It used to be mine, too.'

Mayfly took this small revelation, this glimpse of his childhood self, as an invitation to delve deeper.

'Were you very young when your father died?'

'I wasn't even born. I never knew him.'

'But you still miss him, I guess, do you?'

Rusty had tired himself out on Robby's lap and contented himself quietly with the soothing hand brushing back and forth on his forehead.

'I used to,' Robby said. 'It was kind of weird, missing someone who was just a face in a photograph. It wasn't like he became a ghost; he always was one.'

A silence fell upon them, and Mayfly was afraid her inquisitiveness had gone too far. Aware of midnight's approach, she pictured her parents preparing for their walk to the stones. At this moment, they would be dousing the last of the fire and hanging up the guitar over the back door of Nirvana.

The muffled echo of something falling heavily in the distance, or perhaps of a door slamming, made Robby jump again.

'Is it very serious, your mother's problem?' he asked, in a too-sudden attempt to cover his obvious trepidation.

His question was so unexpected that Mayfly answered without pausing to think. Even as she did so, she knew there was another way for her to say the words than to spit them like grit from her tongue.

'She's dying.'

Robby bent lower, as if something in Rusty's tired movements had drawn his attention.

'She seems so well,' he said. 'So easy in herself.'

'Yeah, and you know why? Because she's trying to make

Bubble feel better, she's trying to make him feel he's not a complete head-case for believing those bloody stones will cure her. Can you believe that?'

'People did believe in that kind of thing once.'

'Not any more. Except for a few throwbacks like Bubble.'

'I never heard anyone play the guitar as well as he does,' Robby said. 'And that voice ....'

'Maybe so, but he never made it, because he didn't have the guts to try,' Mayfly snapped. 'Too busy playing loopy games in his head. Well, I've had enough of his games.'

'You're not going to the stones tonight, then?'

'Not on your life. Not tonight or any other night.'

Hearing yet another soft disturbance outside, Robby stiffened visibly.

'Why do you live with your great-uncle if you're so afraid of him?' Mayfly asked sharply.

'I've no choice,' he said. 'And I'm not afraid of him.'

'Well, you're obviously afraid of something out there. You're getting on my nerves, you're so bloody wired-up.'

Robby shifted Rusty from his lap and placed him on the ground. He tucked the blanket around the dog's soft bulk. Rusty whined tiredly as Robby withdrew his hand and stood up.

'I'm worried about you staying here,' Robby said. 'And it's nothing to do with Eamon. There was a nest of rats in the cottage, last time I was down here. Eamon caught some with these traps he makes.'

'Yeah, right. Any excuse to turf me out.'

Dark as the room was, Mayfly could see the intensity of Robby's look.

'I don't want to get rid of you. I had a good time to-night. I don't often have a good time.'

'I checked out the rooms,' Mayfly said quickly. 'It's not the first time I've had to squat where I don't belong.'

Robby stepped a little closer. He thrust his hands into his pockets.

'I know the feeling,' he said. It was like a song whose words Mayfly had been waiting to hear for a very long time.

ⓒ℈

The campfire was a sodden mass of dampened grey ashes when Robby passed back along the narrow road. Dimly lit, the dormobile stirred briefly like a big, tame creature dreaming of fright. Silently, Robby cursed McCabe's unsettling presence. He was about, Robby felt sure of that. Years of hunting with Rusty had attuned his ears to the slightest disturbance in the fields around Cloghercree. He knew the darting rush of hares; the slow, bulky crawl of badgers; the swift break and sudden wary halt of foxes. McCabe was some unearthly hybrid of all three, a chameleon of the dark.

From the moon's position above the highest of the cemetery pines, Robby guessed at the time. Half past eleven, twenty to twelve at the latest. He headed towards the cemetery. He wasn't quite sure why. Maybe it was the shock of hearing that Mayfly's mother was dying. In the moments of doubt before he'd gone to the campfire, it had been the prospect of meeting her again, of sensing that ease she radiated, that had swayed him. Of course, he'd wanted to see Mayfly, too, and to taste the freedom that the New Agers represented for him. He'd been surprised to find such tension existing among the three, but, in the circumstances, it was understandable. They were a family under pressure, but they were still a family, and that was more than he had.

He was sorry he'd told Mayfly the lie about the rats. He'd had to say something to put her off the cottage, with McCabe hovering around. And yet he hadn't set his own feelings for her aside and demanded, as he should have, that she leave; and that bothered him.

As he drew closer to the cemetery gates, the eerie sense that the dead refuse to go away had never seemed so vivid. He was afraid, and it felt at once ridiculous and wrong-headed — ridiculous because the dead were dead, they couldn't hurt you like the living could; and wrong-headed because it was a terrible thing to fear your own father's spirit. Be angry with him, yes. Curse Sean Wade for dying so young, and for leaving the legacy of his violence, and for drawing his old comrade-in-arms to Cloghercree. But afraid, no. Robby couldn't let that happen. In his determination, he spoke aloud, not caring if McCabe was within earshot.

'I'm not afraid of you,' he said, half-expecting the tall pines to toss their lush branches in answer. But stillness reigned for so long that he wondered whether McCabe had gone away, thinking him mad.

Five minutes later, when he arrived at the house, he was faced with a madness that was only too real.

Before he'd even entered the yard, he heard the low, fevered moan. When he turned the corner of the house he saw, to his surprise, that the kitchen was in darkness. At the far side of the yard, however, a light shone from the garage, and it was from there that the sound came.

Robby crossed the yard and eased back the rattling old galvanised door. The driver's door of the rusty Cortina was slightly ajar. The pale, yellowish glow coming from the car revealed a body slumped on the ground below. A small pool of blood gathered by the head.

Robby moved closer and knelt at the man's side. He held the bloodied head in his hands and leaned over to see the face.

Tommy the Tramp's eyes were closed. Hearing no breath, Robby tore back the layers of coats and sweaters to search for a pulse.

Behind him, the door shot open. 'It's too late,' McCabe

muttered. 'Way too late to be sneaking back home. Where were you, Robby boy?'

With relief, Robby found a pulse in Tommy's neck.

'Why did you have to do this?' he cried.

'Couldn't take a chance. Coulda been anyone.'

'Tommy's harmless. I told you he sleeps in the car sometimes. All you had to do was stay out of his way.'

McCabe sniffed contemptuously and entered the garage. He was carrying the rifle.

'He's asleep now, isn't he? Get outa here and I'll sort him out.'

Robby swung the driver's door out so that it stood between them. The garage was so narrow that there was no space to pass by the barrier. The stale smell of urine and alcohol from Tommy's ragged clothes was overpowering, but Robby got him into the car and pushed him across to the passenger seat.

'What are you playing at?'

'I'm taking him in to the hospital,' Robby said. 'His head is split open. He'll need stitches.'

Keeping a close eye on McCabe, he reached up to the shelf of tools where the spare car keys were always left. He found them quickly and dived into the car, slamming the door behind him. Automatically the car light cut out. It was just about the only part of the car that worked properly. The window on the driver's side hadn't closed for years; there was a gap large enough for McCabe to put his arm through, if he chose.

'Tommy won't remember a thing,' Robby said. 'He never does. He's always too drunk.'

McCabe leaned in through the window. Below, his fingers fidgeted with the door handle. He didn't realise it was clapped out. He could be there all night and never get the knack of opening it.

'Tell us, Robby. Is it something in the blood? Do all the

Wades think they're blessed with nine lives or what, hah?'

'We're not blessed, we're cursed.' Robby told himself to stop talking rubbish and get moving. He fumbled blindly, searching for the ignition.

'What are you raving about?' McCabe, distracted by Robby's words, gave up trying to open the door.

'The stones. My great-great-grandfather thought he could knock them down, and we've been cursed ever since.'

The key slipped into the ignition and he began to turn it slowly. The barrel of the rifle appeared by his temple, the metal tinged with the red of the ignition light.

'Get outa the car. Now. Or you'll be rightly cursed.'

Robby's breath came in throaty flutters. His whole body shook. When the car shuddered into life, he couldn't believe he'd had the nerve to start it. Tommy fell against his shoulder, and Robby didn't have to look to see what caused the dampness on his sleeve.

'He's still losing blood. I'm going,' he said. 'He won't even remember where he was.'

As if of its own accord, the Cortina began to slip forward. Robby was too numb to feel he had any part in its movement.

McCabe withdrew the rifle, but as the tyres touched the cobbled yard, his face was still framed in the window.

'If anything happens, Robby boy, I'll shoot Eamon. Don't think I wouldn't, son.'

'I know you would.'

Robby flicked on the headlights and pressed the accelerator to the floor. At an upstairs window of the house, Eamon's face was briefly lit. An old man, alone in an ancient house, just like he'd be for the rest of his life — if they survived McCabe's stay.

The Cortina hit the lane at thirty miles an hour. After that, the knackered speedometer gave up counting.

chapter 17

Rusty clenched his teeth against the last of the herbal mixture and ducked away from Mayfly's stroking hand. He probably didn't need the herbs now, any more than he needed Mayfly. She brought a chair, the only intact one in the cottage, to the window. Leaning on the windowsill, she waited for Andy and Bubble to make their way to the stones.

When they appeared, she watched them detachedly. Their progress was slow. A midnight stroll, it seemed, with no particular intention, crazy or otherwise. Two old lovers, out under the same moon that had once accompanied their first embrace.

Mayfly was glad she hadn't gone with them. Even spying on them — for that was how it felt — seemed like an intrusion. They had each other, had the shared secret of a life together which had begun long before she was born — there had been ten years between their meeting and her own arrival. These days, all she ever did was disturb their equilibrium.

When Andy had signalled to Robby to follow Mayfly, she'd been secretly pleased. But in the dark cottage kitchen, the scene took on a different meaning. In that gesture, Andy had said, 'We have each other. Mayfly has no one.'

And still she had no one. Robby remained a stranger to her, and there would hardly be time for him to become the friend Mayfly had hoped he'd be. The story of her life.

But not for very much longer. If she could, somehow, keep her sanity through that unthinkable instant of her mother's death, then a different life could begin. Not a better life — certainly not a happier one — but a life that was of her own making.

Mayfly withdrew from the window. Andy and Bubble were still out there. She was alone in the cottage. That was how it was and how it would always be. It almost felt like a new beginning.

CB

'Holy mother o' divine God!' Tommy the Tramp moaned. 'What hit me?'

'You fell, Tommy. You'll be all right.'

Robby already felt he'd panicked unnecessarily. Tommy didn't sound like someone at death's door; his condition certainly wasn't drastic enough to justify provoking McCabe. At least, Robby thought, he'd kept him out of McCabe's clutches. He swung the car into the hospital yard and heard a scraping sound as he slowed down. The exhaust pipe had come loose.

Tommy leaned over and stared into Robby's face, sending out a vile odour of decaying teeth and stale whiskey.

'Sean? Seanie Wade!'

'Robby! It's Robby! Will you ever get it right?'

'Where did I fall?' Tommy asked, oblivious to Robby's irritation.

'I found you near the cemetery, Tommy, remember?'

Tommy shook his head and groaned. He touched his scalp and looked at his wet hand. 'Jaysus, I'm reefed.'

'You'll be fine. They'll stitch you up in here.'

Robby steered into a parking space and jumped out of the car to escape Tommy's scent. Tommy's brain ticked slowly into life. His narrowed eyes considered Robby.

'I could swear I was above in your garage,' he said. 'One minute I was hoppin' into the car, next minute ... next minute, I'm here.'

'You were on the side of the road, Tommy,' Robby insisted, hauling him from the passenger seat.

'But ... but this is the hospital.'

'You need to see a doctor.'

'You know what they'll do to me in there, don't you?' Tommy gasped.

'They'll fix you up. Come on, don't be stubborn,' Robby pleaded, trying to prise the grimy, tobacco-stained fingers from their hold on the car door.

'They'll try to give me a feckin' bath, so they will!'

The stitching took the best part of an hour. Tommy didn't make a good patient. And he had been right: two nurses and a burly Matron took him away for a bath. When he reappeared, slouching between the nurses, his head was covered with a fresh bandage and his clothes had been replaced by a hospital dressing-gown.

'They're keepin' me in,' he told Robby accusingly. With a deep sigh, he added, 'And they're washin' me clothes as well.'

Then, offering Robby the opportunity to make up for his treachery, he asked, 'Any chance of a few bob, Robby?'

When Tommy was looking for money, he always got the name right. Robby still had the three tenners his mother had given him for his birthday, in his pocket. He handed one of them to Tommy.

'Don't go drinking it, Tommy,' he said.

Tommy grabbed the tenner and slipped it into the pocket of his dressing-gown.

'What else would I do with it? Ate it?' he demanded.

CB

Robby pushed open the hospital door and stopped dead. In the sodium-lit forecourt, an unmanned squad car ticked over lazily. Over by the Cortina, Detective Sergeant Healy crouched low to inspect the rickety front bumper. He hadn't yet looked in Robby's direction, but Robby knew he was aware of his presence.

'You brought Tommy in,' Healy said. 'Did you knock him over?'

'No, I found him on the road. Near the cemetery.'

Healy circled the car. He took his time, pausing, edging back, moving on again until he came back to where he'd started. Trailing him, Robby felt he was being drawn into some kind of trap.

'Where were you going? You were out fierce late, weren't you?'

Robby didn't know what was on at the cinema, and if he mentioned 'friends' that could be checked out too — if Healy believed he had any.

'Don't tell me you found yourself a young one.'

And Robby fell for it, knew he had, even while he was falling. 'Yeah, I did. What's it to you?'

'Not a thing. Only I need to know her name.'

'She wasn't with me when I found Tommy.'

'That's all right. I'd like to know all the same,' Healy said. 'Otherwise we'll have to make a trip to the barracks. Sort out your story, like.'

Robby wished Healy would stop inspecting the car, so that he could see his face and guess what was going on in his mind. Healy failed to oblige.

'She's one of the New Agers. Up on the park road. We went for a drive and ....' Robby checked himself. 'And after I dropped her back, I found Tommy.'

Healy gave up the pretence of examining the Cortina, so suddenly that Robby was taken aback.

'What are you doing hanging around with that shower?' he demanded. 'For God's sake, Robby, will you ever get sense! They're being staked out for drugs, that lot.'

'She's not —'

'She's trouble, Robby. All of them are.' Healy clenched his fists in exasperation. 'Will you, for God's sake, go back to your mother! You're going to land yourself in it, one way or the other — with this shower of wasters or with Eamon.'

Robby's silence wasn't deliberate. He was simply dumbfounded by his own naïveté. How could he have imagined it was just ordinary roll-your-own cigarettes Andy and Bubble had been passing between them? And if the guards were watching the New Agers, weren't they likely, eventually, to spot McCabe at the farm? And Robby and Eamon would do time for hiding him ....

It seemed like Robby would never get a better opportunity to get out of the trap he was in. All he had to do was tell Healy the whole story.

Just as he was setting his doubts aside, Healy spoke. The detective couldn't have chosen any words more likely to change Robby's mind.

'You're the very same as him,' he said, motioning Robby to get into the Cortina. Robby guessed what Healy meant — Tommy wasn't the only one who thought he looked like his father. But he was only half right.

'Everything locked up in your head. The worries of the world on your shoulders. Not until the very day he died did I know Sean was in the IRA. I never even suspected it.'

Lifting his cap, Healy rubbed the perspiration from his bald pate. He wasn't playing the detective any more.

'The day he lifted the All-Ireland Minor cup, above in Croke Park, he mentioned me by name. In front of sixty thousand people. Imagine that. I only brought him as far as the Under-14s, but he remembered me on a day like that. I was never as proud in my life. Class, he was. Pure class. Like yourself, Robby, like you could be — and that's no word of a lie.'

Healy leaned in through the car window. His pleading eyes were so close to Robby's, they almost had to cross to find focus.

'Get away from Eamon, Robby, and his bitter old Republican guff. O'Neill told me he offered you a job. Take it.'

The cosy little picture of O'Neill and Healy discussing his future disgusted Robby. He started the car and pulled away before he could dig himself into a deeper hole.

It wasn't easy to stay under thirty miles an hour until he reached the outskirts of town, but he managed it. Then, eyeing the rear-view mirror, he cut loose and covered the mile to Cloghercree faster than he ever had before. Behind the Cortina, sparks shot upwards as the exhaust pipe scraped along the ground.

As Robby steered the car into the garage, he saw the kitchen light come on. He walked towards the house and the kitchen door began to open, sending out a long rectangle of light that turned the cobbles to a faded carpet of welcome. McCabe was peering up at the night sky.

Robby came within three feet of him and started to speak. The fist cracking into his face felt like a slab of metal, sending him firmly to the ground.

'Never — ever — defy me again, son,' McCabe warned.

Inside, Eamon sat by the table. He didn't stir so much as a finger. Robby picked himself up and walked through the kitchen without a word.

Hours passed before he slept. And when he slept, the numbing dream was worse than ever, because this time, he was alone in the white room of his paralysis.

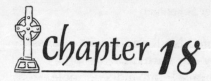
chapter 18

In the storm of spring-cleaning that raged around him, Rusty cowered, his head under his paws. Broken chairs, bits and pieces of splintered wood, shredded curtains, long strips of fallen wallpaper, were flung into the front garden. Then came broken cups and plates; blackened, dented pots; cracked vases full of withered flowers that burst into dust at a touch. The broom raised a thick mist, and the sunlight straggled palely through its density.

Mayfly had started the tidying up in a distracted way. There was no plan to it, and no sense either. What was the point of clearing out a cottage she would never live in? None, except to pass the time in which she should have gone to Nirvana, made the breakfast, talked to Andy, seen what the previous day's exertions had done to her. None, except to blank out the dread from her mind.

With every burst of energy, Mayfly told herself she'd return to the dormobile when this or that corner was cleared. But one thing led to the next, and she went through the two small bedrooms with the same thoroughness. At every turn, she hoped to see Andy standing there, cup and plate in hand. After each disappointment, she threw herself with renewed abandon into her task.

Overwhelmed by the stifling dust of other people's yesterdays, she tired and was seized by an inexplicable panic. If anything had happened to Andy, she knew, Bubble would surely have come running to her. It wasn't that. Perhaps it was simply the fact that there was so little left to do in the cottage. Whatever the cause, she might easily have given in to the sense that everything was futile: the lives lived in this place and beyond, her own wasted morning hours .... It was Rusty who saved her.

The noise and the dust drew him out of hiding. Climbing onto all four legs with some effort, he paused and considered the distance to the door. A little drunkenly, he made his way across the swept floor. Mayfly followed him in silent encouragement.

He tottered out into the sunlight, his red coat dusted grey as though his illness had aged him. His tail swayed back and forth, gently at first, then more excitedly. Mayfly expected him to run from her. Instead, he raised his head, let out a big, healthy bark, and rubbed his coat against her legs. For the first time since her arrival, she really looked at the green fields of Cloghercree and noticed what a beautiful place it was under the midsummer sun.

∞

McCabe wasn't hungry. He pushed the sausages around the plate with his fork, and rubbed the ball of his fist into his eyes. Robby and Eamon had finished eating, and he hadn't yet spoken. Their every movement drew sharp glances from under his brows.

The blackened pouch beneath Robby's right eye throbbed. When he dared to speak, his words were as hushed as a mourner's in church — prayers without much hope of an answer.

'Mam wasn't at home yesterday,' he said. 'I've to go in again today. After I look over the cattle.' He couldn't even remember which field they were in, but they more or less took care of themselves at this time of year anyway.

Below the table, Eamon's boot tapped against Robby's ankle. McCabe shook his head.

'I *have* to go.'

'Your mother can wait,' McCabe said, tossing his fork down on the plate. 'Hasn't she that scumbag O'Neill to take care of her?'

'Tomorrow, maybe,' Eamon suggested, his boot still nudging Robby's ankle.

'Not tomorrow either,' McCabe said. 'Let O'Neill bring her out here and I'll pot him. If it wasn't for him I wouldn't be trapped here. I'd still have plenty of hiding-places.'

Kneading his forehead, elbows on the table, McCabe looked as vulnerable as he was ever likely to be. The rifle lay across the far end of the table, within Robby's reach.

But he considered the possibilities for too long. McCabe looked at him knowingly. 'You've a right shiner there, son. Don't make me give you another one, hah?'

'I have to see my mother. She's ... she had to go to the city for a check-up.'

'Pull the other one,' McCabe snorted. He picked up the rifle, making ready to leave. Eamon's silent nudging was worse than McCabe's dismissal. Robby wanted to hurt his great-uncle, make him suffer.

'She's pregnant,' he said. 'That's why she needed the check-up. I'm afraid there might be something wrong.'

The sounds that came from Eamon were like Rusty's poisoned wheezes. The tension at the table shifted. In an odd way, McCabe, for all his hold over them, was excluded from it.

'Pregnant, Eamon. Expecting a baby, you know?' Robby went on. 'Happens sometimes, when people get married.'

Eamon grabbed his stick as though it might stop his head from spinning. His lips curled. 'The slut,' he said. 'The cheap dolled-up slut.'

Robby kicked his great-uncle's foot away from his, stood up and held his fist to Eamon's face. 'If you ever say anything like that again, I'll kill you.'

'She's a slut and you know it. A slut married to a gurrier. A fine bloody pair.'

'Robby, sit down. Take it handy,' McCabe said, not quite in command. 'And you, Eamon, shut up with that old talk.'

'I've every right to say what I want about her,' Eamon declared. 'She married O'Neill. O'Neill! And now —'

'Belt up, Hopalong, you waste of space you,' Robby interjected furiously. If he'd had that fistful of clay, he'd have stuffed it in Eamon's filthy mouth.

The stick was swinging in Robby's direction before he had time to react. At the last moment, McCabe's rifle whisked it away and across the room.

In his weariness, McCabe looked almost human. So haunted did he seem that ghosts might have been dancing before his eyes. Robby felt sure he was going to break very soon, and he prayed it wouldn't happen in Cloghercree.

'We'll be needing some supplies, anyway, I suppose. Just remember the rules, and no more annoying my head, right?' McCabe warned. 'Will you be seeing O'Neill?'

'Not if I can help it.'

'I meant what I said, Robby boy. If I got half a chance I'd do us all a favour and shoot him.' McCabe's stubbled cheeks were turning a blotchy purple. 'I'm down for life one way or the other, if they catch me.'

'They won't catch you, once you stay on the move,' Eamon said. 'Not that you're not welcome here, but there must be somewhere you can go. A lot of people owe you.'

'No one wants the likes of me any more.' McCabe looked bleakly at Robby, something lost and uncomprehending in his expression. 'Go ahead, Robby. Look after your mother. You only have the one. Even if she is married to a bastard.'

'I'll tidy up first,' Robby said, struck with wonder.

'Eamon'll do that.' McCabe got up from the table, straightened his back stiffly, and rolled his shoulders. 'When you come back,' he said, 'there's something I want you to do for me. We'll talk about it later. Time I checked myself out of this convalescent home.'

He kicked Eamon's stick into the flames of the fire.

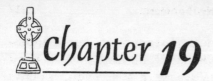# chapter 19

The creak of the front gate brought Mayfly to the cottage window. Andy, she hoped, bringing her lunch. Even the prospect of it being Bubble couldn't dull the appetite she'd worked up. But when she looked out, it was Robby she saw, and her hunger disappeared.

He nuzzled in close to an excited Rusty, his head lowered, his black hair gone spiky from lack of brushing. Mayfly went and leaned against the door-jamb, waiting for him to notice her.

'Did you sleep all right?' Robby asked, still hunched down rubbing noses with Rusty.

Mayfly thought, at first, that he was talking to the dog. Then he glanced up at her and she saw his swollen eye. Her mouth was dry, her tongue felt clumsily big and in the way of what she had to say.

'Yeah. What happened to you?'

'I was fixing the barn roof,' Robby said, hiding in the pretence of play with Rusty. 'The hammer broke. It's nothing.'

He wasn't any better at lying than he was at acting the macho man. Mayfly watched him as his gaze wandered to the pile of rubbish in the front garden.

'You were tidying the place?'

'I hope you don't mind. It was just something to do, you know.'

With Rusty at his heels, Robby went to the cottage door. Mayfly stood aside so that he could see the results of her work.

'You must have been at it all morning,' he enthused. 'It's like it used to be.'

A brief flicker of sadness passed across his features. Then, aware of their unintended closeness, he stepped back. Too urgently, he said, 'We have to talk. There's something I have to tell you.'

The black eye took on a life of its own, fluttering oddly, like the eye of a child attempting to wink. Robby covered the bruised, flickering bulge with his fingers. His good eye focused on Mayfly with difficulty.

'That stuff your parents were smoking at the camp-fire?' he asked. 'It was hash, wasn't it?'

Mayfly felt her stomach sink with disappointment.

'Why do you want to know? If you're looking to get some, then forget it.'

'No, no, it's not that. But listen, the guards are keeping tabs on them. They got a tip-off.'

The sky above the cottage was brushed with small, slow-moving clouds, though the sun was still warm as ever. Ireland would be no different from all the other countries they'd been to. Different uniforms, maybe, different accents, but the same old story. Their last journey together — and even this realisation came drained of all emotion — would end as the others had: in a quick escape from the police or an ignominious send-off.

'It wasn't me,' Robby said desperately.

'Your great-uncle?'

'I don't know .... I'm sorry, I really am — I ....'

'Doesn't matter.' Mayfly shrugged. 'This'll probably be our last night here. Midsummer's Eve. Miracle time at Cloghercree.'

She would have liked to say that nothing really mattered very much; she would have liked Robby to somehow comfort her. But that was romantic nonsense.

His disconsolate look stirred her — that and her un-willingness to see him go: when he went, she'd have to go back to Nirvana. She couldn't avoid Andy forever. And there was this news to deliver to Bubble.

'Were you happy here?' she asked.

'I suppose so,' he said. 'Happy as I could be without a father. Yeah, I was happy.'

'What happened to him? He must have been very young.'

Robby hid his eye again behind his cupped hand.

'He was nineteen,' he said. 'I don't think you'd like me very much if you knew how he died.'

Mayfly wasn't quite sure why — his deep inhalation of breath, like a swimmer's before the dive — but she knew he was going to tell her.

'My father was shot dead in an ambush up in the North. He was part of an IRA unit. They killed a part-time soldier.'

All Mayfly knew about the IRA was that they had planted bombs in London and Manchester and, last year, in Omagh. To her they were remote, heartless monsters, not real people. But there before her stood one of their flesh and blood — the son of a killer.

'I don't believe it's right to — to kill people .... I wasn't even born ....'

'We can't choose our fathers,' Mayfly said. 'None of us can.'

Robby's unexpected look of irritation made her uneasy.

'Don't compare your father to mine,' he said. 'They couldn't have been more different.'

'I wasn't comparing —'

'The life your father's had — the music, the places you've all been .... Furthest I've ever been was Dublin, and that was a day trip. And he's never killed anyone, has he?'

The pat answer — *There's more ways of killing than shooting* — almost tripped off Mayfly's tongue before she realised the crass unfairness of it. The shock of being made to feel small and petty made her sour.

'We live on the dole. Believe me, it's not much fun.'

'Your life seems pretty bloody perfect from where I'm standing.'

'I used to think so too,' Mayfly told him. 'Until I realised I didn't have a future. Until Andy got sick.'

Skittering around Robby's legs, Rusty grew more and more demanding. His playful nips went too far and Robby pushed him away roughly. When the dog whined in dejected misery, Robby called apologetically to him. The cold edge in his voice had disappeared.

He turned to Mayfly. 'I shouldn't have got thick. You've enough to deal with already.'

'You don't have to apologise,' she said. 'I'm not the best of company today.'

'You're always good company,' Robby answered. Covering his unintended advance, he added quickly, 'So you want to settle down somewhere, is it?'

'I suppose, yeah.' Mayfly was beginning to feel dizzied by the swings in the conversation. 'Go to college, maybe; get a job that means something, that matters. Live in a house .... Ordinary things, really. And what about you? You can't stay with your great-uncle. He's hit you, hasn't he? Was it my fault? Because of Rusty?'

'No. I haven't told him yet,' Robby said quickly. 'I hurt myself with the hammer because I'm the one who does all the work around here. Eamon just mopes in front of the fire, crying over my father.'

He looked out at the hedges on the back road, the hilly fields beyond. They seemed to take him somewhere he hadn't been before, to thoughts that struck him with a wide-eyed wonder.

'I won't be driven out of this farm,' he said. 'I always thought I wanted to escape, but I don't. I want to stay and make something of this place again.'

Rusty had decided to forgive Robby, but he demanded attention as a reward.

'Easy, boy,' Robby said. 'I'll tell Eamon about Rusty this evening, OK? I've to go into town now. Tell Bubble to be careful, won't you?'

Mayfly nodded. Rusty followed Robby lazily to the gate, sure he was being taken back to the farm. When Robby closed the gate, the dog looked about him in sad confusion.

'Stay with Mayfly, Rusty,' Robby told him. The sound of her name on his lips made his going more bearable.

Across the short path, they looked at each other, waiting, reluctant to part.

'Mayfly?

'Yeah?'

'Would you like to keep Rusty? I mean, you're the one who cured him.'

'Andy doesn't take to dogs, and we don't have a lot of space in the dormobile,' she said. 'But thanks for the offer. I know he means a lot to you.'

'I'll call later, then. To collect him, OK?'

'Yeah, see you later, Robby,' she said, and she thought, *Yeah, see you later, for the last time.*

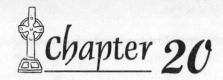# chapter 20

Just because you expect the worst, it doesn't mean you're any better prepared for it. Mayfly had been sure that Andy's boundless energy would burn itself out, and she was proved right. She found Andy sitting on the back steps of the dormobile, looking ahead with dazed, half-closed eyes. Her stare didn't become any less vacant when Mayfly stood before her.

'Andy?' Mayfly whispered, watching the perspiration trickling from beneath the bulky Rasta cap.

'Welcome home, Fly.' Andy hadn't yet focused on her daughter, and it felt like a rebuke. 'You sleep OK?'

At Mayfly's side, Rusty was strangely muted after his delighted scamper from the cottage. Mayfly couldn't see Bubble, but she heard the snap of branches and his mellow singing voice further along the road.

'Yeah,' Mayfly said. 'And you? You seem really tired.'

'You know me,' Andy said flatly. 'Soon as I get it, I spend it. Money, life, the whole damned thing. Phoom, baby, up in smoke.'

She was looking blankly beyond Mayfly, and instinctively Mayfly turned. A few smoky grey clouds were gathering above a line of distant pines, daring to encroach on the sky's blue perfection.

Suddenly Andy was with her again, and the little twist of darkness in her vanished in the wryness of her smile.

'Hey, the herbs really did the trick, man.'

She leaned forward to touch Rusty, faltered and sagged back. Mayfly moved quickly towards her, but Andy regained her balance and raised a defensive palm.

'I'm fine, Fly. No need to jump on me, right?'

'You should be lying down. You know that. So does Bubble.'

Andy let the admonition pass. Her cool equilibrium returned and she gestured to the step where she sat.

'We're going to talk, Fly,' she said with a quiet force. Mayfly went to her, feeling as ready as she could ever be for such a moment.

Andy's arm slipped around her waist, all bone and sharp edges. Rusty sidled away and sat on the grassy margin by the ditch, as though he knew not to intrude. Out of sight, Bubble switched disconcertingly from one tune to the next without a break. Mayfly sensed a desperation in the relentless singing, as though he couldn't allow himself to stop.

'Last night at the stones we talked. Long after, too,' Andy began. 'Talked about you.'

Mayfly blushed, remembering how remote they'd seemed as she watched from the cottage. Yet, all that time, she had been at the centre of their attention. She wondered how much Bubble had told her mother about their unpleasant exchanges.

'This kind of life isn't for you,' Andy said, as though to confirm Mayfly's worst fears. Silencing her objections, she went on, 'Forget the guilt-trips, Mayfly. We want to do what's best for you. I know we should have got around to thinking about all this before. But you get sick and suddenly you're the centre of your own dark little universe, and everything else, everyone else, is out there somewhere on the edge. I shouldn't have let that happen, but I did, and I can't change it. But we can change what comes next.'

No, we can't, Mayfly thought. *What comes next is that Andy dies and then the universe doesn't have a centre, and I'll have to make my way through it somehow, and how am I ever going to do that?*

'You want to get yourself a good education, for a start,' Andy said firmly. 'So the question is, how do we make that possible?'

In turning to look at Andy, Mayfly loosened her mother's hold on her waist. She waited, but Andy's arm remained slack. Her voice, however, gained in strength and was all decisiveness.

'The way we see it, there are two choices. At least, these are the choices we came up with. Maybe you've figured out some others.'

'I haven't thought about it,' Mayfly said. 'Not really.'

Andy watched the approaching clouds, which were too small to pose much of a threat after all. Mayfly thought she was doing it because she had to concentrate so hard on playing this part — the responsible, forward-looking parent. It was a role Mayfly had too often wished she would play. Not any longer.

'Option number one: we stick around in one place for the next few years, so you don't have to keep changing schools. Bubble gets a job, we get an apartment or whatever — somewhere there's space for you to study, have friends over and stuff. For college you can get a grant we'll chip in, naturally — and you could work nights. Not easy, but maybe worth a shot.'

All Mayfly could hear was that repeated 'we'. But there would be no 'we'. In that vague future of which Andy spoke, 'we' meant Mayfly and Bubble — and Mayfly wanted no part of that.

'Option number two,' Andy said. 'No easier, I'm afraid. Not for Bubble. Or for you.'

Mayfly knew what was coming, and she left her mother's side.

'I don't want Sir Gordon Blenthyne's money. What kind of person do you think I am?'

'Hear me out, Fly,' Andy insisted, though she was

already beginning to wilt. Startled by Mayfly's sudden movement and the raised voices, Rusty sprang up and tottered as quickly as he could back along the road towards the cottage. The impulse to follow him was strong, but Mayfly found herself transfixed in the silence that was suddenly emptied of Bubble's singing.

'OK, Bubble walked away from Sir Gordon and his blood money. But we thought, why not put some of that Blenthyne loot to good use? Why not ask Sir Gordon to put you through the best schools and colleges? Then you could go out into the world and make it better in some little way.'

The continuing effort was reducing Andy to a sinking huddle, a flower whose brief opening was almost done.

'Let me help you into bed,' Mayfly said, not caring what 'we' thought, wanting to tell Bubble what she thought of this great act of self-abasement he had proposed on her behalf.

'Don't worry about me, Fly. Promise you'll think it over. Maybe talk to Bubble on the way back tomorrow.'

'We're going tomorrow? But you're not well enough to travel, Andy.'

'Bad vibes here, Fly.' Andy looked towards the Stone Field and the big house among the trees. 'Real bad karma. I hope that kid's going to be all right.'

'Why do you say that?'

'Oh, hell, you know me and my intuitions. Most of the time I get things assways, right?' Andy said. 'Talk to Bubble, OK?'

No doubt Bubble was somewhere nearby, hiding away as he'd hidden from the world all his life. Mayfly felt sure that if she looked hard enough, she'd see a faint plume of smoke signalling his retreat into brain-dead unreality. The prospect of telling him he was being staked out for drugs delighted her.

But Andy hadn't finished yet. When she had, Mayfly's mind was emptied of all vengeful thoughts.

'We watched the dawn come up,' Andy said, as she raised herself and negotiated the steps into Nirvana. 'Guess that's why I'm so whacked out, man. But it was worth it. Sharing the dawn with someone, Fly. It doesn't get any better than that. Pity you weren't there.'

☃

Mayfly found Bubble sitting in the shade of the ditch bordering the Stone Field. There was no squashed joint between his fingers. He was staring, not at the circle of stones, but at the sweep of long grass. Mayfly had the oddest feeling that the calm which Andy was losing had somehow transferred itself to him. She knew that nothing she had to say could hurt him.

'Strange, isn't it?' he said, in a voice which had the mellowness of his singing. 'When you look into the grass for long enough, let your eyes rest, you don't see the blades of grass any more, just this big green haze. It's like your hand would pass right through it, if you tried to touch it. That's how it is, Fly. Every little blade is a life. Yours, mine, Andy's. And all of it, man, it's just one big, beautiful illusion. Beautiful, man.'

When he looked up, Mayfly wondered if all he saw of her was a haze too. She felt invisible in his presence.

'Why did you have to bring up all this Sir Gordon stuff with Andy?' she asked. 'You really think I'm some kind of gold-digger, don't you? All I want is an ordinary life.'

'No, I don't. And, besides, it doesn't matter what I think of you. Or what you think of me. Love has nothing to do with thinking, man. You're my daughter. I'm your father. It's always going to be that way.'

'It didn't stay that way with your family, did it?'

'Looks like that, I suppose,' Bubble acknowledged. 'But I'll always be a Blenthyne. One arms dealer in the family doesn't mean I can't be proud of the name. And I've reasons to be proud. My great-grandfather, for one. Came from nothing, built up a steel company, never forgot where he came from. My grandfather and his two younger brothers, all killed in the Great War. Three Victoria Crosses in one family. Their sister, Maud, spent her entire life as a Christian missionary in China. I don't have to agree with what they did to admire them. Brave people, Fly. You've got that Blenthyne spirit too.'

He contemplated the green field again, and it was like a dismissal. Jealous of his trancelike state, Mayfly needed to break it.

'You've been smoking too much of that —'

'Not today, Fly. Don't need it today.'

'Well, if you have any left, you'd better get rid of it fast. The police are watching you. Robby told me so.'

Her announcement wasn't the body-blow she'd expected it to be. Bubble had no intention of letting go of the magic green carpet before him.

'Just as well we're on our way, then,' he said.

'I wish,' she told him — and it didn't feel like a final push for victory over his impregnable calm, but like just another cry of defeat — 'I wish I didn't have to travel one more bloody mile with you.'

Still, he sat unperturbed.

'You'll go, Fly, but you'll always come back to me. That's how it goes with the ones you love. Just like Andy.'

Running didn't help. The sight of her spruced-up temporary home didn't help. Rusty's presence by the cottage gate didn't help. Mayfly brushed by him and sped along the path, taking his yelping as a greeting and not as the warning it actually was. Inside, a visitor waited.

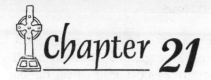

chapter 21

'What I said was —'

'We all say things we don't —'

'I didn't mean to be —'

'I know you didn't —'

In Grace's house, where everything seemed so perfect, where nothing was broken that O'Neill couldn't fix, the only thing that didn't run smoothly was Robby's conversation with his mother. He felt more out of place there than ever. The only consolation was that O'Neill wasn't around. At least, not yet.

'You'll think about the holiday, then?' Grace asked, as she placed the mug of coffee on the matching coaster before him. 'And the job?'

Robby picked up the mug and pretended to lose his answer in the heat of the coffee. At the other side of the table, Grace seemed very flushed after the small effort of filling the cafetière and pouring the coffee. He wished she'd stop staring at his swollen eye.

'Did it go all right? The check-up?' He concentrated on the coffee, as if watching would cool the dark, grainy liquid.

'Oh, it was nothing. Nothing to worry about,' Grace said. With panicky good humour, she added, 'They're more careful about older women in ... in these situations. Imagine, the consultant actually said that. *Older* women! Thirty-five, I am. I was fit to ask him what age *he* was.' Too quickly, her laughter dissolved. 'I'm so glad you came. I miss you, Robby.'

Robby looked up at her, but it was Mayfly he was

seeing. When she was carrying him, Grace had been just a
few years older than the New Age girl. He thought of all
Mayfly must be going through. He thought of all Grace
must have been through back then, facing his birth, facing
the future alone.

'I'll go on the holiday,' he said, thinking that if she only
knew how many 'if's stood between him and that fortnight
in Kenmare, she wouldn't be so close to joyful tears. *If*
McCabe really did check out of 'this convalescent home',
if Robby wasn't in jail for harbouring a psychopath, *if* he
was still alive .... For the moment, all he could hope for
was that Grace would stay on her side of the table and not
lean over to touch his eye, as she seemed to long to do.
'Eamon can manage for a week, I suppose.' *If he's not in
jail. Or dead.*

'I wish I could talk to Eamon,' she said. 'I wish I could
make him understand. He was so good to me when you
were born — giving me the cottage, the money to buy
your cot and everything .... Oh, I know, he probably did it
out of guilt over Sean. But he needn't have; he could have
walked away, like my own family did. And I didn't make
it easy for him. All the time he was helping me, I was
blaming him for what happened to Sean.'

'So why did you take the cottage?' Robby asked. 'Why
didn't you go and live somewhere else?'

'I know I should've gone. But I didn't have the
strength to make a decision like that. And I suppose I
wanted to be in Cloghercree because that's where Sean
was buried. I couldn't imagine a life without him. I
couldn't let go of him.'

Until O'Neill came along, Robby thought. Then it was
bye-bye Sean, and bye-bye Robby. He damped down the
anger rising in him; if he started to let it out there'd be
another scene, and then O'Neill would be chasing out to
Cloghercree like a pit-bull terrier. Then it would be bye-bye

O'Neill, and maybe even bye-bye Grace — how could she cope with losing her man again? And bye-bye, the unborn child.

'Do you think Eamon will ever change, Robby? Liam says he won't, and that's what worries me so much about you being out there. You wouldn't stay if you thought anything ... anything bad was happening out there, would you?'

'Course I wouldn't,' Robby said. 'Anyway, Eamon knows the war is over.'

'Does he, though?' Grace asked. 'He's still full of hate — for me, for Liam .... How can he hate the man who saved his life? Liam went back for him that day, when this McCabe fellow wanted to leave him. How could he forget that?'

O'Neill was lying, but there was no way Robby could tell her he'd heard McCabe's and Eamon's side of the story. And their version had to be true: why else would Eamon feel so indebted to McCabe?

'Liam is worried that McCabe might find his way here,' Grace said. 'He says no one else would take him in. Only Eamon.'

The sound of O'Neill's car pulling into the driveway reached Robby. His mother's pleading expression tore at his heart.

'Don't worry, Mam. I won't eat him,' he assured her. *Not this time.*

They watched as O'Neill, in black overalls, took his time removing his heavy working boots on the patio. The scene was strikingly familiar, and at first Robby imagined he was experiencing one of those odd moments of déjà vu. Then it all came back to him, right down to the smell in the cottage kitchen that long-ago day — the rich, garlicky smell of spaghetti bolognese, his favourite dish.

His twelfth birthday, it was, but the new bike O'Neill had bought him was still leaning against the front wall of the house, the silly ribbons his mother had put on it gone straggly and half-undone. In school, Robby had opened his desk and found an envelope addressed to 'The Incredible Hulk'. Hulk he was: a foot taller than all his classmates, and fat — puppy fat, Grace called it — and awkward as a deranged ape. And dumb. Dumb enough to open the envelope in front of the whole class.

On the front of the card was a cartoon gorilla with Robby's name scrawled above its head. Through watery eyes, he tried to read the many inscriptions inside. Only the largest of them swam into view: 'What's the difference between a big, fat, hairy ape and Robby Wade? None!!!' He looked around the classroom and knew, by the leering faces, who the culprits were.

O'Neill had listened to the tale of woe without a word, his ruddy face growing a deeper red by the minute. This wasn't the first such story he'd heard from Robby. Usually he'd simply assure the boy that his day would come. Robby expected the same thing this time; it was all he wanted, really. What he got was O'Neill's palm across the face — not a hard blow but a stinging, shocking one.

The 'logic' that followed would rankle with Robby for years, partly because it was so corny, partly because it was so true.

'You hit me!'

'You let me hit you.'

'I wasn't ready. It wasn't fair.'

Another slap sent Robby reeling, not with its force but with its unexpectedness. For years afterwards, Robby would blush at the thought of his pathetic reaction. 'You hit me again!' he squealed. He went at O'Neill with flailing arms, but his blows were fended off with an ease that enraged him even further. 'I'll kill you! I'll kill the whole shaggin' lot of them!'

When he gave up, he was blubbering like the big slob he knew himself to be, and O'Neill held him until Robby stopped trying to push him off.

'That means nothing, Robby. Talk like that and you're the one who'll get hurt. What did you just learn when I hit you?'

'Leave me alone. I hate you.'

'Two lessons, Robby. Always be ready. And never get angry.'

Then he taught Robby how to box, fair and hard. In six months, he'd sorted the bullies. That was the third lesson. Wait — wait so long they think they're waiting to trap you.

O'Neill opened the door and paused for a moment. Robby thought of McCabe — another believer in reverse psychology. His mind was doing somersaults. Who'd know better than O'Neill how to handle this situation? And Robby didn't have to like him to ask his help, did he? He felt like a twelve-year-old again, ready and willing to be told how to sort out his tormentor.

Then O'Neill spoke, and it was like that long-ago slap all over again.

'There's a coincidence,' O'Neill said. 'I spent half the afternoon out in Cloghercree.'

After the fright came the absurd fantasy that O'Neill was going to say he'd confronted McCabe and put him away ....

'Fixing Mick Johnston's bailer,' O'Neill explained. 'What happened to your eye, Robby?'

'I was just telling Mam,' Robby said. 'I nearly finished myself off with a hammer on the shed roof.'

'Robby ....' O'Neill began; but Robby started talking like he'd never talked to them since their engagement.

When he left, he'd promised not only to go to Kerry with them, but to take the job at the garage and to think about moving in with them. He even discussed names they might give the baby. He was cracking up, and the harder he tried, the more he was convinced that O'Neill wasn't fooled.

'Or, if it's a girl, what about something really different?' he said, in the middle of all this craziness. 'Something like ... something like Mayfly.'

They all laughed, but inside, he was weeping.

૱

Back at Cloghercree, Eamon told Robby he hadn't seen McCabe all afternoon. After that they didn't speak. Their thoughts, Robby knew, were filled with the same question: was McCabe gone for good? It seemed like a foolish hope, but every hour that passed was a further reason to believe in it.

Robby spent the evening in his bedroom, listening to Jeff Buckley, but the music didn't touch him as it usually did — only the high plaintiveness of that voice from the dead.

The evening grew dark, and McCabe still hadn't come to tell Robby what task he'd had in mind for him. Finally, a torturous balance tipped over in Robby's mind. His longing to be with Mayfly outweighed the risks of leaving the house. He slid open his bedroom window and descended into the starry cavern of Midsummer's Eve.

Chapter 22

An hour after Robby had arrived at the cottage, they'd hardly spoken at all. Rusty, exhausted, lay immobile beneath his blanket. Mayfly and Robby were restive, filled with an energy that couldn't find words to express itself. Mayfly couldn't remember how the nervousness had begun, but she blamed Robby — his over-reaction to every small sound, his eyes wide and alert in the light from the uncurtained window. She didn't quite know what she'd expected from his visit, but she was disappointed anyway.

'Your great-uncle called here today,' she said. 'He was nice as pie, told me I could stay here as long as I wanted.'

'Eamon was here?'

'Yeah. He seems kind of young to be your great-uncle. And what's with that big green tattoo? Kind of over the top, isn't it?'

'He got it done when he was young and it won't come off,' Robby answered uncomfortably. 'Did he say anything else?'

'Well, he said he was happy to see Rusty. But I don't think Rusty was over the moon about seeing him.'

'Is that all?'

'Yeah, except he seemed to know we were, like, friends,' Mayfly said. 'Why was he snooping around here, Robby?'

'He often comes down to ... to check the traps and stuff. He forgets where he's set them, or else I've found them and thrown them in the cellar up at the house. They're too dangerous to have about, with people coming to see the stones and all .... He's not a dangerous man. He just does stupid things.'

His sudden volubility felt like a diversion, and Mayfly remembered Andy's concern for him.

'Are you going to be all right here?' she asked. 'I'm worried about you.'

'I can take care of myself,' Robby said hastily. 'I just have a few things to sort out.'

'Things you haven't told me about.'

He shrugged but made no answer. A long silence descended on them.

'Do you have any idea yet when you're leaving?' Robby asked.

'Tomorrow. Is that soon enough for you?'

'Too soon. It's good to have someone around ... someone to talk to.'

That made both of them laugh — they'd made such hard work of talking at all. And in the long exchange that followed, that spirit of lightness prevailed over all their worries.

In the end, it was the tones of their voices, their harmony, that mattered, not the stories they had to tell. Their fears and uncertainties didn't miraculously resolve themselves; but sharing them with each other was an answer in itself.

For this reason, perhaps, they went to the stones with Andy and Bubble. There was no big discussion, no explanation; they simply went, Rusty scampering alongside them under the perfect moon. Then they returned to the cottage and talked some more.

But the promises to write, to keep in touch, to maybe meet again next summer, threatened to spoil all that had gone before. Even the tentative plan to meet briefly the next day, before Mayfly left, seemed wrong-headed. Tacitly, they agreed it was better not to. This night together was enough, and more than they'd expected to have. And it hadn't yet ended.

Mayfly took off her wet Docs and, fully dressed, slipped into her sleeping-bag to get some heat back into her bones. Robby stood at the window, as though he was on guard or uncertain what he should do next. Rusty jumped excitedly about Robby, fired up at the prospect of returning to the farm with him at last.

'I should let you get to sleep,' Robby said, daring to peer over his shoulder.

Mayfly didn't answer. She didn't know how to. Since their return, the cottage had become a different place. When they left, it had been someone else's; now, somehow, it was theirs forever.

Robby bent down to calm Rusty. He was within touching distance of Mayfly. All he had to do was reach his hand across to touch her face. His eyes sought permission and it came. They kissed.

'Stay a while longer,' she said, and his arm was her pillow.

CB

Hours, minutes, seconds aren't real. They're man's invention, a crude measurement of time's passing. But every individual mind measures differently. Time flies when you're having fun. Time drags when you're bored. Time is away and somewhere else when you're high on some bright emotion. Transcendence, they call it. The mind transcends time and silences the dull, heavy ticking of the clocks we make of ourselves.

Robby had read all of that in a book he'd borrowed from the town library a year before. It was supposed to be a detective story, but it turned out the hero fancied himself as a bit of a philosopher. Only now, way past, beyond, above midnight in the Stone Field on Midsummer's Eve, did the fictional detective's ramblings make complete sense to him. If there was a secret to this business of living, it was in finding ways to escape the trap of hours, minutes and seconds.

It happened sometimes when he listened to music. The first time he'd heard Jeff Buckley's album *Grace* on his Walkman. At Bubble's impromptu concert by the camp-fire. Or at the cinema, when some film swept him along and ninety minutes went by in a flash. And it had hap-pened that night with Mayfly at the cottage.

Sure, there had been moments when the fear had seeped back in, but they had passed. Or it had been easier to set them aside until later, because when he was with Mayfly, 'later' meant as little as those bits of man-made time.

When he'd left she was sleeping. Her eyelashes flick-ered and he was sure she was dreaming. He wondered if he might be in her dream. The very thought was amazing — at once to be sitting beside this sleeping girl and to be with her in her imagined places.

During that timeless interlude, the skies had opened. The earth, parched from weeks of sun, swallowed the puddles of rain greedily. Robby's combats flapped wetly against his ankles as he walked through the long grass towards the stone circle.

He heard the click of the rifle's catch first. Then he saw the long moonshadow move, separate itself from the shadows of the stones. McCabe stood on the high ground, rifle at the ready. Stock-still, a statue, waiting.

Robby anticipated the questions, the simmering anger in the asking. He had every right to be terrified, every right to be devastated at the thought of Mayfly's departure the next day. Instead, he approached McCabe without a check in his stride, blundering like a badger walking into one of Eamon's traps whose deadliness was beyond his comprehension. Even Rusty knew better; he kept his distance, heading for the gate the long way round.

'Nice of you to show up,' McCabe snapped. 'You said you were going to bed. You lied to me, son. *Nobody* lies to me. That bastard I kidnapped tried it, and I cut his ear off.'

When the bullying at school had been at its worst, Robby had lain in bed thinking of smart answers he could deliver when he was confronted. In the real situations that followed, he had been just his old self again, sinking in mute self-pity. Now, as he walked the steep incline and leaned on one of the stones near McCabe, he could almost believe in miracles. He knew what to say and how to say it, the exact tone of voice to use, the precise mixture of truth and lies that was required to deflect McCabe's anger. He didn't feel like he was either a hero or a coward, and he didn't care one way or the other.

'It wasn't you I was lying to, Razor,' he said. 'I was lying to Eamon. I went looking for you to tell you where I was going, but you were with him. He'd crack up if he thought I was meeting Mayfly.'

'Mayfly?'

'You know who I mean.' Robby worked up a smile. 'The New Age girl. You were talking to her earlier.'

McCabe's grip on the rifle was loosening. Once in his life, the day Grace and O'Neill had married, Robby had got drunk, and it had felt just like this — until he'd got so sick that Eamon had had to call a doctor.

'I think I'm in love, Razor, and she's leaving. What am I going to do?'

'What are you feeding me all this crap for?' McCabe blustered. 'What I want to know is —'

'Who else can I talk to?' Robby pleaded, squeezing out a tear. 'Eamon? He treats me like dirt, Razor. He tells you how wonderful I am, but you know what he told me the other day? He said I wasn't fit to be called a Wade. I can't even talk to my mother any more. Not while she's married to O'Neill. What am I going to do?'

It was time to draw back a little; to throw in a brief, anguished pause; to bow his head as though he was about to break down. These things were easy to do, because so much of what he was saying was true.

'I love her, Razor. I don't know what I'll do without her.'

'Forget about her, Robby boy,' McCabe said gruffly. 'Next town she moves on to, she'll have another young fellow. They're all the same, the women. Take it from someone who knows.'

These odd flourishes of humanity — the Santa Claus story, his declaration that 'you only have the one mother', this hint of a past love in his life — were somehow more disturbing than the aggression and the threats.

'Anyway, you have a busy day ahead of you tomorrow, hah?' McCabe said. 'You won't have time to be mooning over young ones. I want you to go to Clare for me.'

'Clare?'

'Is that a problem?'

'No,' Robby said. 'None at all. What do you want me to do?'

'It's my last chance, Robby, the only way out I can think of,' McCabe said; and there was that human face again, in all its dangerous desperation. 'Don't screw it up on me, right?'

&#x03;

It was no longer Robby whose arm cradled Mayfly, but Bubble, and she was a child again. Beneath her, the cottage floor had dissolved into sand, and a balmy night breeze swept up from shimmering Mediterranean waters. Bubble was telling her the story of how he had come by his nickname, in Los Angeles, back in the early 70s. It had been the bedside story of Mayfly's childhood; later it had become the campfire story which helped her to forget about police and suspicious natives.

Inside, Mayfly protested; but when her turn came to join in as she always had, she couldn't stop herself.

Bubble delivered the story in a mournful, put-upon Texan drawl.

'Seems like only yesterday when Terry Blenthyne set out from good old London town in his psychedelic T-shirt, with a banged-up geetar slung over his shoulder. He was gonna be the next Bob Dylan. He was gonna be a songster with a message. And he was gonna make a few bucks on the side. So he hits L.A. Or L.A. hits him. He plays the bars, the ratty clubs, busks the boulevards, waits for Destiny to come a knock-knock-knocking on his ....'

'Door, door, door!' *Mayfly chimed in.*

'But Destiny's got better things to do, and meanwhile, young Terry's down to his last cup of coffee. So he tells hisself, "If the Man don't come to me for my music, I gotta go to the Man." Puts a tape together of all his sad old songs. Gets the address of a recording studio on ... on ....'

'Sy-ca-more Avenue!'

In the dream, night turned suddenly to day. Beneath Mayfly, the warm sand had transformed itself to stone, cold and grey as the Prague sky above. They were sitting on the Charles Bridge, among the portrait painters and the puppeteers and the strolling tourists. Below them, the Vltava River was the mucky brown of Rusty's herbal brew.

'So he walks down the avenue,' *Bubble continued.* 'Makes his play at the reception desk, and his sad old smile melts the heart of the Ice Lady there and she says ....'

'"Wait in the waiting room for the Man!"'

'"Well, thank you kindly, ma'am, I've waited this long, guess I can wait some more." Then — whoosh — the door opens. In comes the Man — whoosh — bald, red-faced, in a major hurry. "Name's Johnny Younger. Younger yesterday. Younger tomorrow — if I don't get a goddam heart attack in between."

'So he asks Terry if he wants to make a few easy bucks. "But my songs, ain't you gonna listen to my songs?" "Later," says Mr Younger. "Meanwhile, you wanna make that money or not?" Terry doesn't like the sound of this, but he's got two *choices: play the geetar or eat the geetar. "You want me to do backing for someone?" he asks. "What kind of music we talkin' here? Folk, funk, soul, country and western?"'*

'*Bubble-gum music!*' *Mayfly cried, with an enthusiasm she couldn't feel.*

Now they were in Marrakesh, and the evening sun cast a brilliant orange light over the teeming market on Djemaa el Fna. Close by, a snake charmer stared with hypnotic eyes at a hissing serpent uncoiling itself upwards. A wizened old man in a ragged robe sat cross-legged and arranged his wares — an assortment of dentures of all shapes and sizes. A band of travelling drummers pounded out the heartbeat of the souk.

'"*Goes like this*," *Mr Younger says.* "*We lay down a backing track — nice, upbeat, poppy stuff, boom-boom, ding-a-dong, whatever. Then we get a couple of guys to sing real slow on tape, got it? Then we speed up the tape, make it fast to fit in with the backing track. And these guys sound like goddam monkeys or something. Kids go crazy for it. Hundred fifty dollars in your pocket, plus I listen real good to your songs. Deal?*"'

'*Don't take it, don't take it!*' *Mayfly pleaded, though her voice remained playful.*

It was night again, and they were at the standing stones of Cloghercree. The moon hovered grossly, a cracked and peeling eyeball, seeming to advance threateningly.

'"*Hundred fifty bucks, wow*," *Terry tells hisself. But then the little voice in his hair says,* "*What about your reputation, man?*" *Then his stomach rumbles and he says,* "*You gotta deal, Mr Younger.*" *Plays the gig, record sells a million, but he never gets more than the hundred fifty and Mr Younger never listens to his songs. Plus, the guys he hangs out with take to calling him Bubble, and no one takes Terry Blenthyne seriously any more. Was he sad? Man, he was sad ....*

'*But every story's got an angel, right? And this one's got Andrea the Angel ....*'

'*Andy!*'

ন্ধ

She woke calling her mother's name, not in dreamy rapture but in bleak desperation. The echo of Bubble's voice hung in the air — the voice that had fooled Andy into loving him and had fooled Mayfly too. The voice that, if the dream had lasted, would have gone on to say, 'And Andy taught good old Terry Blenthyne that loving was more important than writing songs about love.'

Robby was gone. Mayfly placed her fingers on her dry lips. His absence was like a thirst.

chapter 23

In the outhouse garage, Robby and McCabe prepared the old Cortina for the journey to Clare. Rusty cowered under the work-bench, silenced by McCabe's threatening glances. Robby topped up the Cortina's oil and water and tested the fan belt's tightness, knowing straight off it would have to be replaced. McCabe, meanwhile, scrupulously cleaned Tommy the Tramp's blood from the passenger seat. He whistled tunelessly; he seemed fresher, this early morning, than he had since his arrival.

'Can you give me a hand here?' Robby called, taking down a new fan belt from the supply they kept on the garage shelves. He had the job down to a fine art, taking half as long as an experienced mechanic would have. McCabe followed his instructions and watched him work. He was impressed. When Robby slammed down the bonnet, he said as much.

'Habit,' Robby said. 'I better get moving.'

'It's going to work out, Robby. It has to. Otherwise it's on to Plan B, hah?'

'What's Plan B?'

'Haven't a bull's notion, but I'm working on it.'

As the car moved out of the garage, McCabe gave Robby the thumbs-up, his hand covered in dark flakes of dried blood. Out in the yard, Robby looked in the rear-view mirror. McCabe was smiling, not a cynical smile but an almost fatherly one, and it chilled Robby.

He took the back roads out of Cloghercree and away from the town. After twenty minutes, he reached the main road and pushed the Cortina as hard as he could, remembering

Eamon's parting words in the kitchen: 'Mind the car.'

The miles flowed by quickly. The further Robby travelled, the more determined he became that no one was going to push him out of Cloghercree — not Eamon nor McCabe nor anyone else. He was a Wade and Cloghercree was his birthright. After McCabe was gone, things would change at the farm. Robby would make them change. He'd use blackmail if he had to: his silence about McCabe in exchange for the right to run the farm. Then he'd get rid of the cattle and make an organic farm of it. Bubble had been right that night at the campfire: all that organic food was hard to get, and there was sure to be a big market for it.

As he neared the fishing village of Dunmore South, Robby wondered how Sean Wade had passed the last night of his life. Had he talked with Grace, into the early hours, of some vague future? Had he kissed her, knowing that all the while he was keeping his terrible secret from her? Had he not realised that his very love for her would keep her a prisoner for years to come? He must have done. Robby was three years younger than Sean had been, and he knew that love and lies didn't mix.

Dunmore South was a picture-postcard village. A narrow, winding main street descended towards the pier, flanked by flower-bedecked houses painted all the colours of summer. To the right, a couple of side-streets branched up into the hills. Robby turned the Cortina down the third street and parked twenty yards along, just as McCabe had instructed. Everything was going so smoothly, he felt sure it was going to work out.

As soon as he opened the car door, the sea air hit him, tinctured with salt spray and the sweet, heady corruption of seaweed. He thought it might even be worth putting up with O'Neill to get down to Kerry and wake up to this brain-clearing blast every morning for a fortnight. Along the main street, day-tripping parents chastised ice-cream-messy kids. A couple of local heavies stood on a corner, watching sourly as the tourists tramped around their village. A pair of old ladies, weighed down with shopping bags, blocked the footpath for a chat.

Robby found the sweet-shop McCabe had mentioned, O'Mahoney's, and went inside. Following McCabe's carefully-laid-out plan, he dawdled at the rack of postcards and watched the street for any suspicious natives. He felt he should buy something besides a card with an out-of-date shot of Dunmore South — 'a souvenir for me,' McCabe had said. Robby guessed it was to be proof that he'd actually gone there. He bought a packet of wine gums, the first things that came to hand.

As Robby walked on, the sea came into view, in all its polished granite vastness. His stomach fluttered as though he were another excited child among all the others. In a way, he was. The waves whispered to him, as they did to them, of freedom.

At the pier, he sauntered along, trying to look disinterested as he searched for the *Saint Brigid* among the docked fishing boats. The men, sitting on upturned wooden crates as they mended nets and lobster pots, took no notice of him. At least, they appeared not to; but the further Robby walked, the more certain he became that his every move was being monitored.

He reached the end of the pier and turned back, scrutinising the boats' names again. A voice called from behind him.

'Are you looking for someone?'

Robby turned to face a small, wizened man wrapped up in oils and gumboots as though for a winter gale.

'The skipper of the *Saint Brigid*.'

'I thought you might be,' the man said. 'You're looking at him.'

'But where's the boat?'

The fisherman pointed out to sea and told him, with a wry chuckle, 'Ten miles out, son. And twenty fathoms down. Lost her two years ago.' His hooded eyes closed a little more. 'What do you want me for?'

'I've a message from Mr Sharpe,' Robby said. (*'My cover name. Good one, hah? Razor Sharpe.'*) It seemed pointless, now that McCabe's hopes for a passage to France were literally sunk. 'But you don't have a boat, so ....'

'Oh, I've a boat, all right. A new one. But *Mr Sharpe* won't be boarding her. Tell him that. Tell him if he comes next nor near Dunmore South, we'll dump him in the middle of the Atlantic with a concrete block for an anchor.'

'He said you owed him a favour,' Robby said desperately.

The sailor moved past him and stooped to check a set of lobster pots nearby. 'Mr Sharpe isn't owed any favour by any of us. And if you've any sense, you'll wash your hands of him, son.'

'It's not that easy.'

'There's only one way to deal with the likes of him, son. And whatever you do, don't miss with the first shot.'

Robby sensed that the man was signalling with his averted eyes to someone on the main street above. His instinct told him to get away from Dunmore South as quickly as he could.

In a claustrophobic panic, he dodged in and out against the flow of holiday-makers descending the sharp incline of the street. Faces bore down upon him, innocent conversations turned to conspiratorial whispers. As he approached the corner into the side-street, he felt certain that the Cortina wouldn't be there, that whoever the fisherman had signalled to would be lying in wait for him.

When he saw the car, he broke into a run, got himself inside and sped out of the village. Potholes jarred his passage as he drove, his eyes on the rear-view mirror more often than on the road ahead.

After a few miles, when he was satisfied he hadn't been followed, he steered the car down a narrow lane leading to a cove and watched the sea all afternoon.

If McCabe didn't have a Plan B, neither did Robby. Nor did he spend those hours working on one.

Instead he remembered, in every detail, the holidays he and Grace had spent in places like Dunmore South. He remembered a photograph she'd taken on a beach like this one: a three-year-old Robby walking alone, his shadow long with evening, hands joined behind his back in a curiously adult way. 'My little man,' Grace called that photo. Robby recalled how, in later years, O'Neill would sometimes join them for the day and play hurling with him along the damp-packed sand; recalled even the hard slap of his bare feet on that sand that should have hurt but never did, no matter how long they played. He imagined walking the beach below him with Mayfly, and knew real pain.

When the dread came, the dread of the inevitable violent end to McCabe's stay at Cloghercree, it came disguised in pangs of hunger. Robby took the sweets from his pocket. Wine gums. When he was a child, they'd been his favourite sweets, because Grace had once told him they'd been his father's favourites. Everyone who ever claimed to care about Robby bought him wine gums — Grace, O'Neill, even penny-pinching Eamon.

He opened the car door and tossed the sweet packet in among the scrubby tufts of wild sea-grass in the sand dunes.

chapter 24

What surprised Mayfly was not the number of squad cars that surrounded Nirvana but the suddenness of their appearance on the back road. There were no tell-tale sirens or flashing lights, no megaphone histrionics like that time in Greece; nothing but a polite knock on the dormobile door and an evenly delivered warning to Bubble, Andy and Mayfly to remain sitting while the search went on. They found the small block of cannabis resin, hardly bigger than a worn-down school eraser, in the cupboard under the sink. They took Bubble away while they turned Nirvana upside down looking for another stash.

Mayfly sat on the bed holding a dazed and tearful Andy. She was afraid of what this raid would do to her mother, but she couldn't bring herself to feel angry with Bubble for causing it. He'd ignored her warning, but she didn't imagine Andy would have heeded it either. And it wasn't as if Bubble was going to be locked up for a thimbleful of hash. He'd get a warning, a fine maybe, or an invitation to leave the country. She tried to reassure her mother with that thought.

'Why don't they leave us alone?' Andy answered plaintively. 'Why can't they ever leave us alone? We've never done anyone any harm. Anyone but ourselves.'

'They're doing their job. There's a law, and they ....'

Andy pulled away from her and watched in mounting rage as the guards invaded every corner of the dormobile, like birds of prey in the belly of a dead beast. All the colourful fabrics they had collected on their travels seemed drained, suffused with the same pale grey as Andy's face.

'You can be so bloody cold, Mayfly,' she cried. 'You don't care that Bubble is banged up in the police station, do you?'

'I warned him. Robby told me he was being watched,' Mayfly said, her heart thumping. 'It's his own fault.'

'Fault, fault, fault. Everything's gotta be someone's fault with you.'

'Things don't just happen.'

'Goddammit, Fly, I'm sick of all this crap you're laying on us. Making Bubble out to be some kind of goddam monster. Making little of us and the good times we had, the stuff we did. And all because we got no cash flow, because we didn't spend our lives thinking about tomorrow and tomorrow. Like you weren't a happy kid, Fly? Like we beat the crap out of you, did we? I'm goddam sick of you. First you treat me like a goddam invalid — won't let me cook, wash up, nothing. Then you treat me like I'm already dead. You spend your day trying to avoid me —'

'I came to the stones last night,' Mayfly said. It was the only thing she could think of that she'd done for Andy in the past few days.

'Thanks a bunch, Fly. I should be grateful for that, should I? That's supposed to make up for ... for this negative goddam aura you're spewing out all over us, when we're trying to — to keep our heads together, man ....'

Andy's eyes, burning into her, frightened Mayfly at first. Then they set off some petulant spark within her that blazed out of control. Even the presence of the guards couldn't dampen the fire in her.

'And I'm sick of you, Andy, and Bubble too. All I ever get from either of you is dumb hippie clichés. And the past, yesterday, yesterday, yesterday. And all this fake laid-back calm, when you're just as afraid as I am, and all your dumb philosophies and religions aren't worth a damn now when they're supposed to matter. And Bubble with his dumb bubble-gum-music story, making excuses for himself —'

'The story's true,' Andy snapped. 'But he didn't take that bubble-gum money because he was hungry, he took it because *I* needed it. And you know what for? Heroin. Yeah, I was a junkie, and he believed the story I fed him about needing cash to check into a clinic. I took the money and I split. Didn't see him for three years. Not until he found me in Newark, living like a rat in a beat-up apartment house, and he rescued me. From myself, Fly.'

For Mayfly it was one of those moments when you know the earth is revolving because the inside of your head is revolving with it. Confused, embarrassed, shamed, she stared down the young guard who was obviously more interested in what Andy had to say than in searching the black plastic bag in his hand.

'I always thought you'd been together since '72,' she said. 'That's what you told me.'

'Bubble didn't want to lay that stuff on you, but that's how it was. Look at those photos you've got; you won't find any from '73 to '76. He never made it in the music game because he took three years off to find me, and after that he was a nurse and a prison officer to me for a couple more years. Why d'you reckon you didn't come along until '83, Fly? Because I wasn't clean until then. If you'd been born before that, you'd have been born a goddam junkie.'

'You should've told me. Bubble should have ....'

'You should have known, Fly, you should have known he was one of the good guys. And I don't care if you think that's another of my hippie clichés. So we didn't solve the problems of the world? So we didn't find some religion or whatever that explained everything? We did our bit, Fly, and we picked up a few words of wisdom along the way and tried to live them, tried to pass them on to you. What the hell else do you expect of us?'

'Andy, please, you're going to make yourself —'

'One last thing, one last thing,' Andy insisted, struggling against the dizziness that had her teetering dangerously on the edge of the bed. 'Why did I come here? Why did I follow Bubble's dream of the stones? Not for the miracle. Bubble gave me the miracle before you were born, Fly. I came to give him something after all he's given me.'

The guard looked up from the plastic bag he'd finished emptying, book by book.

'I've to search under that bed,' he said. 'You'll have to wait outside.'

'There isn't any more hash here,' Mayfly shouted. 'We're not running a bloody junk shop!'

'Is that so? Then how come your father tried to sell it to the young lad on the farm up there?'

When Andy crumpled to the floor, she made as little noise as the empty plastic bag falling from the young guard's hand.

೮೩

Robby steered the Cortina into the back road. The dor-mobile was gone. He'd known it would be, but he'd needed to go down there, to feel the last remnant of her presence in the late evening air. He was sorry he had. It felt as though the scorched circle in the roadside grass was burnt into his soul.

At speed, he reversed the car along the lane. Then, in-stead of turning right towards the house, he headed for the cemetery. He wondered whether you could be arrested for what he had in mind. What would the charge be? Breaking and entering?

The car wasn't travelling very fast when it hit the cemetery gates, snapping the big rusted padlock with a steely twang. In the sudden glare of the headlights, the polished gravestones flashed like the eyes of the waking dead. Robby threw the switch, plunging them into the dusk again. He didn't need the light to know where his father's grave stood. His heart raced, but he felt nothing beyond the determination to do what he'd set out to do.

Up ahead, the lane veered sharply to the right. Robby didn't turn the steering wheel. The dark outline of the high Celtic cross lay before him, less than twenty yards away. It took a minute or two to sort out the seat-belt; it hadn't been used in years, if ever. He raised the hand-brake to rein in the latent speed he was building up. He heard himself say goodbye to his father.

His timing was perfect. In the same instant, the head-lights came on and the handbrake was released. Just before he hit the high gravestone, he thought it would fall on the car, on him. The seat-belt snapped on impact, and Robby flung his arms out to stop himself being thrown through the windscreen. But the windscreen held, and so did the gravestone. Even the car's engine purred bliss-fully on.

Robby climbed out of the car, pressing his hand to the painful twinge in his neck. The high cross had been loos-ened from its plinth; only the car's dented front held it in place. He climbed onto the bonnet and began to heave against the stone cross.

He was weak from the shock of the crash, and his efforts came to nothing. He tried to summon the strength of hate, tried cursing his bloody murdering father, but Sean Wade was stone cold dead. He tried to tell the part-time soldier that he was doing this for him, but Alan Wilson was dead too. Robby was crying for all the dead — Bloody Sunday, Enniskillen, Omagh — knowing that for him the slaugh-ter wasn't over yet. McCabe was trapped in Cloghercree. He wasn't going to give himself up; that wasn't his style.

He'd try to fight his way out, as he had at the kidnap
scene. And as long as he had the gun, Robby and Eamon
were his hostages.

The big cross shifted a little and Robby paused for
breath, keeping his weight against it. So it was back to the
gun, back to the Action Man stuff again. Mayfly couldn't
have known how appropriate the nickname was, how
inescapable Sean Wade's chosen path was for his son.

As he prepared himself for the final push on the cross,
Robby remembered Eamon's tearful description of Sean
Wade's heroics in that long-ago All-Ireland Minor Final.

*'Two minutes to go, it's level pegging and we're under
wicked pressure. Sean battles for this ball out in midfield, right
by the sideline. Three lads around him, swinging the hurleys
like butchers' cleavers — you could hear the timber cracking off
his ankles. But, by Jesus, he whipped back into them, took lumps
off them and got the ball up in his hand. His back to the goal-
posts, on the halfway line, mind you. And over his shoulder he
hits it, left-handed. And it sails, by God, it sails! Knocking
corners off the clouds, it was. And then down it came, straight
between the posts. After the match I asks him how he did it. Do
you know what he said? He said, "The more wallops I got, the
more I was thinking: we can't lose, I can't let that happen. And
then I got the ball in my fist and I knew I had to use it, so I just
let fly." God, he was something else. He could have been ....'*

When — if — Robby somehow got possession of the
rifle, he would 'have to use it'. The monument to Sean
Wade gave way beneath Robby's shoulder and collapsed
into the bed of white crystallised pebbles below. There
was another part to his plan, but he didn't have the stomach for it now. In any case, where would he find a couple
of small timber planks to sling together in a makeshift
cross, or something with which to scrawl his father's
name — just the name, no stupid epitaph — across the
horizontal bar?

He got back into the Cortina. As he drove towards the house, steam began to billow so thickly from under the bonnet that it was like driving through a swirling fog. He knew he'd cracked the radiator and that, by driving on, he could screw up the whole engine. He didn't care.

Halfway along the lane to the farm, the car stuttered to a halt. Walking towards the house, Robby expected McCabe to materialise from the dark fields at any moment, but he was inside the cobbled yard before he encountered him. When he did, his stomach lurched, but there was nothing in there to throw up.

Instead of a gun, McCabe was wielding a bloodied shovel. On the cobbles lay what was left of Rusty — a twitching, dismembered mess of torn flesh and splintered bone.

chapter 25

Sometimes, as Robby walked from town to Cloghercree, he'd come upon a fox or a badger which had been crushed under the wheels of a passing car. He would cross to the other side of the road, avert his eyes and try to sing some tune aloud. As he walked past McCabe and the remains of Rusty, the same emotions — fear, revulsion, the little daredevil voice in his head saying, 'Look! Look!' — clawed at his insides. Instead of music, however, silent deliberation carried him past the appalling sight in the yard.

McCabe didn't have the rifle with him. The kitchen door was open, suggesting he'd emerged from there. There was a chance, a reasonable chance, that the rifle might be in the kitchen.

'That bloody animal turned on me, Robby,' McCabe growled. 'Nearly took the leg off me.'

Robby reached the door. Inside, Eamon stumbled to a sudden halt near the table. There, newly-oiled and glistening blackly, lay the rifle. Closing the door quietly behind him, Robby moved forward. They heard the muted clang of the shovel falling on the cobbles.

'For the love of God, Robby, don't pick it up.'

'You should have told Sean that, seventeen years ago,' Robby said. He grasped the rifle. 'It's too bloody late now, Eamon. This is where your heroics in Fermanagh got us.'

McCabe was shouting as he swung the door open.

'Robby! What did the skipper say? Don't tell me you couldn't find him, 'cause if you do, I'll ....'

It was clear that McCabe had looked down the wrong end of a gun before. He didn't panic, didn't even seem surprised. He smiled and raised his hands in a mocking gesture of surrender.

'So, my old pal the skipper let me down, did he?'

'He said they'd throw you in the sea if you ever went near Dunmore South,' Robby told him.

McCabe nodded and lowered his arms slowly.

'Leave your hands out where I can see them,' Robby ordered.

'What's the plan, Robby? You going to shoot me?'

'If I have to.'

The kitchen, always so dreary, seemed shockingly bright — bright as the white room of Robby's nightmare. His hands, too, seemed as numb as they did in that dream, though he gripped the rifle, white-knuckled and unwavering. His mind and body were unwilling, or unable, to make the next move.

McCabe had no such qualms. With exaggerated caution, he went down on one knee and clasped his hands together before him. He looked up at Eamon, dismissing the rifle as his glance swept by it.

'What have you to say about this, Eamon?' McCabe asked. 'I saved your skin, remember?'

'I don't remember anything,' Eamon said. 'I was unconscious.'

'I went back for you. I saved your bloody life, you ungrateful —'

'One of ye did. I don't know which one.'

'You believe O'Neill saved you? The man who ran off with Sean's girl?' McCabe snarled.

'I didn't say that. All I'm saying is ....' Eamon said. 'Look, Razor, I told him not to pick up the —'

'Shut up, Eamon,' Robby shouted.

'Ah now, you wouldn't shoot a man before he had time to say a few prayers, would you, hah?'

'Would you?' Robby asked, but McCabe's sneering

tone unsettled him further. Already the rifle was less steady in his hands.

He hadn't noticed Eamon moving closer to him. When the hand touched his shoulder, Robby's fingers tightened instinctively on the trigger. For a moment, McCabe's composure threatened to dissolve.

'Back off, Eamon. You're making the lad nervous.'

The swollen pouches of fatigue below McCabe's eyes quivered. His stare held none of its usual intensity. The harsh features had a frozen, corpselike vacancy. It wasn't pity that loosened Robby's trigger finger; it was an over-whelming sense that he was looking into the beckoning emptiness of a killer's soul.

'Get out, McCabe,' he said. 'Get out of Cloghercree and don't come back.'

The sound that came from McCabe was like the snort of a rearing horse. Eamon made a stumbling effort to step into the firing line, but Robby jostled him away.

'Get out,' Robby yelled, raising the rifle, taking aim.

'Wouldn't that be nice and handy for you, Robby boy, hah? That way you wouldn't have to shoot me. I walk out the door and you can wash your hands of me, right? Well, forget it, son. I'm not going. I don't have anywhere to go. So I'll tell you what I'll do. I'll walk over there to you, boy, and I'll take that rifle off you. Then I'll think about whether or not I'll kick the living daylights out of you.'

'Robby,' Eamon pleaded. 'Give me the gun.'

McCabe had begun his stealthy advance.

'That's right, Robby boy. This is men's work. Give the rifle to the hero of Fermanagh. The man who broke his leg for Ireland. He'll do the job,' he said.

'Razor, the lad doesn't know what he's doing, he's —'

'Ah, he knows all right.' McCabe was standing in front of the table now, and Robby had sidled back around to the other side. 'He knows what he *wants* to do, but he doesn't have the guts to do it. Like father, like son, hah?'

'What ...?' Eamon gasped. 'What are you saying about Sean? Sean was ....'

At last, some trace of emotion filtered back into McCabe's face. It was pure hatred, spiced with bitterness.

'Sean was a hero, a martyr, hah? I'll tell you what he was. What took him so long to fire the first shot, Eamon? He froze, didn't he? Froze so long he made a bloody target of himself. Sean was a gutless piece of shite who got himself shot because he lost his nerve.'

The trigger snapped under Robby's finger. There was no shot, just a loud metallic click that froze all three of them to the spot. Robby didn't know which was worse: the terror of McCabe's reaction or the knowledge that he had been capable of pulling the trigger without thinking.

He composed himself sufficiently to realise he still had the rifle, even if it wasn't loaded. He could wield it like McCabe had wielded the shovel out in the yard, like Sean Wade had wielded the hurley in the All-Ireland Minor Final.

'Fair dues to you, boy,' McCabe said, raising one foot onto the chair beside him. 'I didn't think you had it in you. D'ye know, Eamon might be right. I don't know are you a Wade at all. I wonder was your mother shacking up with some other lad, was she two-timing the brave Sean and he off dying for Ireland?'

Robby swung the rifle, but McCabe ducked beneath the table. When he came up, laughing coarsely, he had a pistol in his hand.

'Remember the old reverse psychology, Robby, hah?' he laughed. 'I carry the rifle everywhere with me, so you think I don't have another gun and the rifle must be loaded, right?'

'He didn't mean to fire at you, Razor,' Eamon interjected weakly. 'He's only a lad.'

'Eamon,' McCabe said. 'You have one bad leg already, don't make me wreck the other one.'

McCabe sat down at the table and gestured with the pistol for Robby to sit opposite him. As unpredictable as ever, he slipped the pistol into his belt and sat back, stretching his arms lazily. Then he leaned forward on the table, tapping out the gentlest of rhythms with his grimy fingers, the nails bitten down to the raw flesh.

'I don't know what I'm going to do with you, boy,' he said, studying the bumpy contours of the tablecloth. 'I let you come and go as you pleased these last few days. And this is my reward. You know, earlier on this evening, when the guards were swarming all over the place, the first thing that occurred to me was that you ratted on me. And do you know something? I was sorry afterwards — actually sorry I doubted you, like. Once I knew it was the hippies they were moving in on, I thought to myself, "I can trust that young lad."'

'What?' Robby blurted out. 'They arrested them?'

'Yeah, they got a tip-off about drugs, didn't they, Eamon? Someone thought it'd be a good idea to tell the guards that the hippies were after offering drugs to a young lad in Cloghercree. Isn't that right, Eamon?'

By the fireplace, Eamon supported himself against the high mantelpiece. He shrugged, but his face betrayed him.

'You said they tried to sell drugs to me?' Robby exclaimed.

He made to leave the table, but McCabe whipped out the pistol and pointed it at him. 'Don't push me, Robby. You're damn lucky to be alive this minute.'

The pistol shook in McCabe's fist, and he pressed his free hand to his arm to steady it.

Robby was well used to feeling trapped, but never, except in his recurring dream, had he felt such complete helplessness. He hardly knew what he was saying.

'But Mayfly ... Mayfly doesn't do any of that stuff. What ... what will she think of me now? How can I tell her it's not true ...?'

'Mayfly?' Eamon muttered. 'What kind of a name is that? Who —'

'His girlfriend, Eamon, one of them knackers,' McCabe told him. 'The guards didn't take your little knacker princess, Robby boy. She went in the ambulance with her mother. Well, I suppose it was her mother. You never know with that crowd, do you, hah?'

McCabe's gibes couldn't hurt Robby.

'Her mother is dying. Her father's in the barracks. She's —'

'Enough, Robby. Spare me the sob story,' McCabe snapped. 'You're not going anywhere, so don't even ask. D'ye think I wouldn't prefer to be off gallivanting with some quare one, instead of being stuck in this hole with people I can't trust?'

He banged his fist on the table, banged it again and continued banging. The gun, in his other hand, wavered dangerously before Robby.

'How the hell did I end up like this, in a kip like this, with no one to turn to?' McCabe wasn't addressing his two prisoners any more. His tone had a curious edge of surprise, of shocked self-discovery, as though he'd never asked himself these questions, or any others, before. He was like a man blinded and scarred in some horrific accident, seeing for the first time the extent of his disfigurement.

'Twelve years old, I was, when I was kicked out of school. 1966 — the fiftieth anniversary of the Easter Rising. And the greatest thing a fellow could do, we were told, was to die for Ireland like Patrick Pearse and James Connolly and the rest of them. So when the Troubles started, what else was I going to do only join the IRA?'

'You did right. You served the cause well, in your time.

Like we all did,' Eamon said, desperate to appease McCabe.

'Shut your bloody mouth, Eamon! You broke your leg, that was your contribution. But me? I did some quare things for them over the years. Following orders, I was, from lads that are walking around in suits now, above in the North, talking about democracy and sitting down for tea and bloody cucumber sandwiches with the Brits. Bloody traitors, the lot of them. And I was turfed out of the IRA because I kept over a few bob after the odd bank job and O'Neill couldn't keep his mouth shut about it. *He* wasn't kicked and punched and lacerated until he was fifteen and big enough to belt back at his father. *He* didn't have to go down to the corner shop for credit for his mother, so he could eat, and then be told to "shag off out of that, your father'll never pay us back".'

McCabe wiped spittle from his mouth and looked at them shamefacedly. His eyes were filled with tears, and Robby saw that this man was desperately afraid. Not of him or of Eamon or of the guards, or of any other human force. Razor McCabe was damned before God and he knew it, knew that his excuses rang hollow for all their passion.

'No, my father wasn't one for paying things back,' McCabe added. 'But I am.'

He stood up and ordered Robby to his feet.

'You're sleeping in the cellar until I decide what to do with you,' he said. 'Eamon, get a blanket and throw it on the cellar floor for him.'

'But, Razor, the cellar's reeking with damp and there's no light — no windows, even.'

'Yeah, well, he should have thought of that before he turned on me,' McCabe said. 'Sure, can't he pretend he's lying on the cottage floor with the young knacker one? Or pretend he's snuggling up to Rusty, hah?'

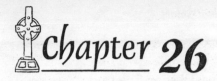

'You have to let him out,' Mayfly screamed into the phone at the hospital reception desk. 'I've been here three hours and she hasn't woken. For God's sake, I've told you, it's serious ..... Serious, you dummy .... I'm not being smart, I'm being angry, you —'

From behind her, an ebony-skinned hand gently took the receiver from her hand. The doctor signalled to the matronly nurse behind the desk to take Mayfly aside. His voice was a broad, measured baritone, speaking firmly to the guard at the other end of the line.

'Dr Rasheed here. I am told there is a problem with releasing Mr Blenthyne .... Yes, that I am aware of .... Well, let me speak to Detective Sergeant Healy then .... Yes, now.'

The nurse led Mayfly to a seat nearby. She felt like an arctic explorer in a snowstorm, dizzily blinded and cold. When she sat down, she thought she was sinking into that brightness. The nurse held her, offering coffee.

'We only drink herbal teas,' Mayfly said mechanically.

'Well, there's a coincidence. I'm on the herbal tea myself,' the nurse confided. 'For my diet, you see.'

At the desk, Dr Rasheed became more agitated, though his voice remained hushed. Mayfly knew she should be at Andy's side, but every moment she spent with her felt like a moment stolen from Bubble.

Like an earnest grandmother, the nurse returned with the tea and insisted that Mayfly drink it, though she had no inclination to.

At last Dr Rasheed put the phone down. He looked drawn and tired, his eyes bloodshot from lack of sleep. He sat down beside Mayfly and allowed a trace of optimism to show in his face.

'Your father will be released soon,' he said. 'Very soon, I hope.'

'Don't they understand how serious it is?'

'They do now. But there are formalities,' he told her. 'And you, Miss Blenthyne? Do you understand what is happening— what might, I am afraid, very well happen?'

Mayfly couldn't answer. Her mind was a blizzard in a No-Man's Land, though she knew what lay beyond.

ભ

In the Intensive Care Unit, a small, insufficient miracle was offered to Mayfly. Andy came to — briefly, but with at least the strength, or perhaps simply the sheer will, to speak. The flashing white graph of her heartbeat was the only measure of time in that room.

Through all her grief, Mayfly thought of Bubble and of keeping Andy awake for him.

'Fly,' Andy whispered, struggling to keep her eyes open. 'Where's Bubble? Didn't get back from town yet, huh? That guy. Bet he's picking flowers along the way.'

Some part of Andy's mind was already going, Mayfly thought: the part that grapples with reality in all its sordid detail. Andy didn't know where she was or how she'd got there. The argument, the guard's revelation about Robby — both Mayfly's fault — had been emptied from Andy's thoughts like heavy objects thrown overboard to keep a boat afloat. Mayfly couldn't let her drift away. She craved forgiveness too much.

'Andy you're in hospital. And I put you here,' she cried. 'We had a terrible row.'

Her mother's eyes closed, and Mayfly grasped the small hand on the bedcovers.

'Andy, please, can you hear me?'

She felt the pressure of Andy's grip, a pressure that

belied her bird-like frailty. At the open door, Dr Rasheed called softly to the nurse who was about to rush into the room, and they disappeared from view.

'Man, can I hear you. Turn down the volume, OK?' Andy said. 'We had a spat, did we?'

'It was awful. I —'

'I guess I told you what a pain in the butt you could be, right?' Andy asked. 'And you told me I was a bigger pain?'

'You remember,' Mayfly said weakly.

'Naw, but I'm glad it happened.'

'But, Andy, if I hadn't got mad, you wouldn't be —'

'Don't be crazy. I been making myself angrier than a polecat. I needed that blow-up. I was losing my way, man, losing my peace of mind. I was ....'

The rhythm of the graph on the monitor changed. It halted for a moment; then it began to move again, but more slowly now.

'I told you about me and Bubble? The bubble-gum money?' Andy asked in a whisper.

'Yeah,' Mayfly answered, swallowing hard, trying not to be afraid, not to let her fear show in her hold on her mother's hand, not to let her tears fall on that hand. 'One of the good guys.'

'The best of the good guys,' Andy murmured. 'Tell him ....'

'He'll be here real soon, Andy.'

'Tell him we made it, Fly.'

Andy's lips came together, to rest there in peace. A little sigh, a minuscule raising of the fingertips, a last touch. It was over.

Through the storm of blinding silence, Mayfly heard footsteps in the corridor. She looked up, but it wasn't Bubble. Dr Rasheed shook his head. Regret and anger deepened his voice still further.

'I'm sorry,' he said. 'They come only now with your father.'

Every moment was terrible. Time dragged Mayfly reluctantly on and on, second by painful second, beyond Andy's passing. She thought that the instant of seeing Bubble would undo her entirely. His tread was unmistakable as he bounded up the hospital steps and sprinted along the corridor, and every step was a nail hammered into her head. She kissed her mother's hand and pleaded, 'Help me, Andy, help us.'

Bubble was in the room, a huge, anguished presence, his throaty sobs reverberating through her. He stood at the foot of the bed and held the iron bedstead. The whole frame shook with the power of his grief. Slowly he began to fold in upon himself, and it seemed like a prelude to some screaming, incoherent collapse of mind and body.

Mayfly took her hand from her mother's, and it didn't feel like the final letting-go she had feared it would be. She went and wrapped her arms around Bubble. He pressed closer to her, his great shudders of pain and loneliness matched in their intensity by Mayfly's own. Together, they swayed, letting the tears flow, exchanging kindnesses.

'I tried to keep her talking until you came.'

'You did so much for her, Fly.'

'She said, we made it, Bubble. She said to tell you, we made it.'

'All three of us, Fly, we made it, man.'

They sat by Andy for a very long time. They didn't speak. They remembered: all the good times, all Andy's goodness, her calm. They re-lived each moment over and again, as though to burn them so deep into their minds that their recollections would never be less than complete.

Outside, the green pigment of the trees returned, leaf by leaf. The sky greyed, lightened, seeming to lift. A pale yellow tinge moved from the far horizon, shaded impossibly to a dappled pink and then a sheer red, spread upwards and outwards. Every rainbow shade Mayfly had ever dreamed of seemed to conspire until the sun erupted in all its majesty. The room was aglow and Andy's face turned to gold.

'She's not gone, Fly,' Bubble said. 'Andy hasn't drifted away to some big Nowhere. She's everywhere now. Always will be.'

Love, in all its joy and sadness, lit up his blue eyes. Watching him and Andy smile as one, Mayfly touched his shoulder and left the room. They needed to be alone. The least she could do was to give them that.

ೞ

She walked along the corridor. The hospital day was already beginning: the rattle of breakfast trolleys being prepared, the smell of toast and fried food, the early-morning banter of nurses and orderlies. It had all been so much easier to bear back in that room, back in that still centre of hard-won peace and raw affection.

She walked down the stairs towards the front lobby. She felt as if she was plunging into the massive indifference that was the morning. Her composure withered in its cold and, suddenly bereft, she seemed to lose the very power of thought.

She walked and walked, a wandering stray, a small lost thing in a vast, empty place. She walked without knowing where she was going, because she was no longer even aware that she was walking.

chapter 27

The long grass in the cottage grove floundered under the weight of dew, but the dry earth beneath was packed tight. Digging was hard work, and the chill of the early morning soon passed from Robby's hands. On guard a little way off, McCabe leaned tiredly against the wizened trunk of an oak tree. He stared ahead sourly, disregarding Robby and the hempen sack from which Rusty's paws protruded. Out of sight, at the hedge between the Stone Field and the back road, Eamon watched for intruders.

'Hurry it up there,' McCabe called. 'You're not burying a bloody elephant.'

'I'm nearly finished,' Robby answered sharply.

'You can say that again, boy.'

Robby vented his frustration on the dry clay, slicing great gouges in it, breaking the bigger lumps with the flat of the shovel. All night, the sense of humiliation had paralysed him more than any dream could. He thought he'd never have that dream again. Nothing could be more nightmarish than these past few hours.

'Are you done or what?' McCabe asked.

'Yeah, I'm done.'

'Well, throw the bloody sack in the hole and get on with it.'

Robby bent down to pick up the damp sack which had seemed so unbelievably heavy as he'd carried it down through the Stone Field. He heard Eamon's voice ringing across from beyond the hedges.

'Clear off out of that! Go on, off with you!'

There was no answer, or none that was audible. Robby

turned to McCabe, but he'd disappeared somewhere behind the ranks of trees circling the grove.

'I'm telling you now! Clear off! Clear off!'

Robby followed the rustle of branches and undergrowth as it drew nearer. When Mayfly emerged into the clearing, he was standing with the sack in his arms. He tried foolishly to hide the open end, but Mayfly's gaze had already fallen on it. This wasn't the same girl who'd charged into the grove, a few short days before, with the fire of righteousness burning in her, all sharp-tongued and vividly beautiful. She was still beautiful, but she seemed somehow lifeless, the spirit dulled in her.

'Rusty got knocked down by a car,' Robby muttered.

Behind her, Eamon limped hurriedly through the back gate of the cottage.

'You're trespassing, Miss. Come on, out with you.'

He made to grab Mayfly, but Robby shouted fiercely, 'She was just about to go, Eamon. Don't touch her. I'm warning you.'

Very slowly, Mayfly stepped back and stared at Eamon. The realisation seemed to take an age to dawn on her. The thicket of trees behind Robby was swept as if by the light morning breeze.

Mayfly looked at Robby again. 'Andy's dead,' she said dully. 'Bubble was arrested because someone accused him of selling hash, and —'

'It wasn't me,' Robby told her. 'It was that scumbag.'

'Robby?' she asked, as though it was of little importance, as though nothing that concerned him was of any real importance to her any more. 'If this is your great-uncle, who was the guy with the tattoo?'

The snap of the rifle's breach resounded through the grove. There wasn't time to warn Mayfly off before McCabe stepped into the clearing. Eamon caught hold of Mayfly. Stirred to life at last, she fought to break free from him.

'Good man, Eamon,' McCabe jeered. 'What would I do without you?'

'Let her go, Eamon,' Robby yelled, lowering the sack quickly into the earth.

'I can't, you know I can't. She'll go straight to the guards.'

As McCabe rushed from the verge of the grove, Robby grabbed the shovel. He spun around and swung hard, catching McCabe on the shoulder. The rifle went spinning to the ground, but McCabe kicked out and Robby took the full force of his boot on the back of his neck. He made a desperate lunge towards the rifle and took another blow to the stomach. Then the pistol was jammed to his temple. As Mayfly screamed, Robby saw, from the corner of his eye, the trigger going back and back and not stopping until the bone-shuddering echo of an empty click darted through his brain.

'The old reverse psychology, Robby boy,' McCabe said, clutching a fistful of Robby's hair. 'This time the rifle's loaded but, lucky for you, the pistol isn't. Lucky for me, too. I need you alive. For now.'

He cracked the pistol into Robby's side. Robby felt nothing, not even the touch of Mayfly's hand on his face, though he saw her there. He couldn't speak, but he pressed towards her. A loud hissing gathered in his head and he passed out.

അ

In the damp, murky pit of the cellar, Mayfly's pleas, her appeals, her screams all went unanswered. In the end her voice gave out. She sat back against the rough, un-plastered brick wall and drew Robby to her. His breath was harsh and laboured, and his mouth oozed spittle. The world was more than indifferent, it was unspeakably cruel. She thought of Bubble, alone at the hospital, wondering whether his daughter had already carried out her promise to walk away from him.

Above her, the incoherent voices of their captors rose and fell in heated debate. The tension thickened with each renewal of the argument.

Eventually, a loud thud put an end to the disagreement — and woke Robby. He tried to sit up but grasped his side and slumped back into Mayfly's lap.

'Did they hurt you, Mayfly?' he asked, and she thought he might lose consciousness again from the effort.

'No,' she said. 'Even if they did, I don't think I'd feel a thing.'

Again, Robby struggled upward. This time he managed to get himself seated beside Mayfly.

'I think he cracked my ribs.'

'Who is he, Robby? What's going on here?'

He told her straight. The whole story, from the farm-yard in Fermanagh to that moment in the cellar.

'I should have forced you to leave right at the start,' he said. 'But I fooled myself into believing you'd be safe, that he'd just move on. I didn't want to see you go, Mayfly.'

'Robby, you couldn't have forced me to go. Nobody forces me to do anything. It gets my back up.'

'But I was stupid, selfish.'

'Yeah, you were. Join the club, Robby. I'm already in it.'

'We'll make it out of here, Mayfly,' he insisted. 'I don't know how, but I know we will, I know it. I'll do anything, anything to get you out.'

She took his hand and pressed it to her face. *I know we will, I know it* — words as meaningless as those stones in their irregular circle, perhaps, but Mayfly believed them, because she had to. That was what it came down to in the end. Belief came not from certainty but from necessity. You believed, not because something was true, but because it had to be.

Hours passed, marked only by the sporadic outbursts of arguing in the house above. Sometimes the noise was

so great that it seemed there must be more than two
people there, and Mayfly imagined that she and Robby
were about to be rescued. Instead, the intervening silences
thickened through the old house, stifling her hopes. Her
eyes felt heavy, but whenever she let them close she saw
Andy and Bubble, in that ethereal blue light, and she
wept quietly.

All the while, Robby's arm enfolded her, and it was
this comfort that finally tipped her over the precipice into
some approximation of sleep.

ઝ

Light flashed across Robby's dark-adapted eyes. Beside
him, Mayfly woke with a start. When she leaned against
him, arrows of pain shot through his ribcage, but he held
on to her.

'Here's the man will save ye, lads,' McCabe declared,
his arm around Eamon's throat. 'The Cloghercree Cow-
boy, hah?'

He pushed Eamon to the floor. The battered face was a
picture of defeat. Then the cellar door slammed shut and
erased it. Robby didn't move from where he sat. He felt
no pity for his great-uncle and no gratitude for the
knowledge that Eamon had, at last, made a stand against
McCabe.

'Robby,' Eamon muttered. 'I tried.'

'Too bloody late,' Robby replied. 'You watched him
hammer me — twice. You didn't lift a finger. You
wouldn't let Mayfly go back to the hospital. How do you
think she feels? How do you think her father feels? Whatever McCabe did to you, you deserved it.'

'I know, I know. I wish to God he'd finished me off
altogether.'

Soon Eamon's form took shape, a pathetic thing carved
out of the darkness. His knees drawn up to his stomach,
Eamon lay like a baby in the womb, afraid to be born into

the world. The silence in the house above and the silence in the cellar were clouds of threat approaching each other with catastrophic intent.

'Robby, I never meant those things I said to you,' Eamon moaned. 'About you not being a Wade. I always meant the farm to be yours.'

'I don't believe you, Eamon. So don't waste your breath.'

'I know I let it go to rack and ruin. But I was never cut out for farming, Robby. I always had it in my head to give the place over to Sean when he finished school; but he was like me, he didn't want this kind of life either. He wanted to go away to college and ....'

His voice cracked with a phlegmy hiss. Robby was almost disappointed as the pause lengthened. Eamon's talk of Sean had always been about the myth, not about this reality he'd begun to reveal.

The squirming form turned further in upon itself and then uncoiled, tried pitifully to raise itself.

'Why did I go persuading him to try out the farming for a year and see if he'd take to it? Why didn't I let him go off to university? He'd be alive today if I had.' All of his gruff reserve was gone, leaving only a thin, hurt whimper. 'And I'd no business letting you stay, Robby. Jealous, I was, plain jealous. Taking you from her, just to take something from her. Same reason I convinced myself it was McCabe who came back for me and not O'Neill. God help me for being such an eejit, but I wanted to marry your mother long before O'Neill came along, only I was afraid to ask her. I was afraid it'd be a slight on Sean's memory.'

The unlikely dream made Eamon seem infinitely more pathetic. A middle-aged wreck on a stick and a beautiful young girl: the very image was a sad joke.

'Soon as O'Neill came around, I knew they'd hit it off. Whatever interest I'd had in the farm, I lost it rightly then.

But I couldn't let go of it, I couldn't make myself say straight out that it was yours. I know Sean didn't even want the place, but saying it was yours made it seem so bloody final, Robby. It was like admitting Sean would never come back. I know that must sound awful foolish. But I lost everything above in Fermanagh, and every scrap of sense along with it.'

'You lost every scrap of sense before you went to Fermanagh. Both of you,' Robby said. 'But at least he was only a young fellow. You were nearly forty years old, Eamon. How could you lead your own nephew into something like that?'

Eamon had struggled onto his elbows. Even in the dim light, Robby could see by his pale intensity that the battle to stay upright was nothing compared to the one raging behind those bruised and tear-stained eyes.

'I followed Sean into the IRA. I'm not blaming him. We did what we thought was right. You have to understand, Robby, it was the time of the hunger strikes. We were all fired up, watching the telly — those poor lads dying, one by one, and Maggie Thatcher letting them die like the hard, cold bitch she was. I thought ... I thought I could keep an eye on him, Robby, mind him ....'

'You didn't make much of a fist of it, did you? He still ended up in Fermanagh with a gun in his hand,' Robby told him, knowing he should be keeping his voice down but not caring. 'Why the hell did they have to drag the two of you all the way up from Cloghercree to do their dirty work?'

'It was chance, pure chance,' Eamon said. 'We were up in this training camp in Sligo, and Sean was .... They never saw anyone so sharp, so keen. I was fit myself, that time, and strong — but Sean, he was something else, and so ... in control, so calm. It just happened they were planning the Fermanagh thing and they changed the team.

They picked Sean, and I said no way was he going unless I was in it too. After that, we just did what we were told to do. That's all it was.'

'Just following orders, Mein Führer. Like the boys in Omagh. And don't tell me that was different.'

Robby's chest ached with heaving convulsions. Mayfly wiped the sweat from his forehead and he realised that his T-shirt was soaked through. White pinpricks of light swam before his eyes and he seemed to be spinning downwards, though he was still sitting propped against the wall.

'For Ireland only!' he shouted. 'Three thousand people, Eamon. All because a few of you decided the gun was the only answer.'

'We didn't *decide*! It happened. We got drawn in. We weren't the only ones with guns. How many did the Brits kill, and the RUC, and the UFF and the UVF and —'

'Save your excuses for Saint Peter, Eamon. See what he makes of them.'

The ceiling shook under a clamour of racing thuds, and within seconds the cellar door was drawn sharply back. McCabe's presence was a force disturbed from the deepest pits of the earth.

'Robby! Out here now!'

'Don't hurt him, please, don't hurt him,' Mayfly pleaded.

'Look at it this way, son,' McCabe said, and the quiet force of his sudden amusement was frightening. 'I'm your Santa Claus, right? Except this Santa Claus cuts a different deal. This Santa Claus gives you two gifts — the girl and the cripple. But you have to give him one in return. Some bastard Santa Claus is, hah?'

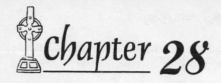# Chapter 28

'There's nowhere left for me to go, simple as that. Never was, I suppose. I never really believed the skipper would help me. But you try, you know, you try to pretend people will do right by you; even when, all your whole bloody life, they never have. The things I did for them. The bullets I sank into men's heads, Jesus Christ, with a big black plastic sack ready to catch the blood — you tie it here, here at the waist, so it won't spill out .... You do all that and then they don't want to know you. And it's all down to O'Neill. I'll never get this chance again, to get him back for what happened. I want O'Neill. And if you want that pair in the cellar to walk free, you'll bring him to me. It's all the same who I kill now. I'm down for life, one way or the other. Down for life. If they get me alive.'

The twists of McCabe's cold logic followed Robby all the way to town. Worm-passages, they were, and he was the worm. His mind squirmed under the shovel-slice of doubt. Was it really just one life he was trading for two others? What if Grace lost the baby? What if she lost the balance of her mind? Even if she stayed sane, how could she ever forgive him?

At the front gate of Grace's house, Robby steeled himself. O'Neill wasn't guiltless. He'd played his part in the murder of Alan Wilson. It wasn't Robby's fault that he would be made to pay for that action. And Grace would survive. She'd survived before. Even the unborn child would. Robby had.

He rang the doorbell and waited. Suddenly aware of how ragged and filthy his clothes were, he tried to rub some of the clay and cellar filth off of his T-shirt and combats.

The door opened. O'Neill, with his garage overalls and oil-stained hands, was as unkempt as Robby himself. His usually ruddy complexion had been reduced to an unhealthy puce. Robby knew instinctively that something was wrong with Grace. He wanted to rush past O'Neill to find her. All along, he'd known that he would need a clear head to carry out this terrible task, but that was becoming impossible.

'Is she all right?' he asked, pressing back the urge to shout.

'You're not to be worrying, now,' O'Neill said, but he couldn't hide his own concern. 'There's a bit of a problem with the baby. There's a chance she might —'

'Where is she?'

'Upstairs. She's sleeping. Go on up to her.'

How could he refuse, though he knew that every step he took might be a step away from Mayfly?

'Don't be afraid, Robby. She'll be .... It mightn't be what the doctors think,' O'Neill said, misinterpreting Robby's hesitation. 'She'll be going into hospital tomorrow. Just a precaution — her age and all .... They're careful about these things.'

'What things?'

'Septicaemia, they think. Some kind of blood poisoning,' O'Neill told him with difficulty. 'And she's all upset over what's been happening.'

In other circumstances, this remark would have been enough to start a blazing row between them. Now, Robby could only listen and take the punishment he deserved.

At first, it seemed he would be spared.

'I don't mean the hassle we had, you and me. That's sorted out, right? But there's some weird stuff going on, Robby, and I can't make sense of it.'

Robby wished he could sit down for even a few minutes. His whole body was shot through with pain and his head ached with this overload of torment.

'The other day,' O'Neill explained, 'someone tried to break in here and knocked down the arch outside. I thought, yeah, well, lots of people have burglars, and these guys get thick when they can't break in, so they do some damage. Then, this morning, we had a visit from the guards. Robby, you might as well know now; you're going to find out anyway. Someone smashed up Sean's grave. Grace couldn't deal with it.'

'I'll go up,' Robby said, summoning up his last reserves of strength. It occurred to him that he could have sacrificed Eamon's life during these past few days, and then things wouldn't have come to this. He wished he had, and that wish had not even the power to surprise or disturb him.

He held his nerve all the way up the stairs, and even while he eased open Grace's bedroom door. Then he saw her. The girlish face, glistening as though washed with the lightest film of sea-spray; the slight round of her stomach rising and falling, rising and falling, beneath the cotton sheet. He felt the breath gushing from his lungs, his knees weakening, carrying him back until he staggered against the landing rail.

Downstairs in the hallway again, Robby couldn't remember how he'd got there. But O'Neill's arm was over his shoulder and he guessed he must have been guided down.

'Don't be blaming yourself,' O'Neill said. In a sudden panic, Robby tried to recall what he might have said during that lapse.

O'Neill squeezed his shoulder to comfort him. Robby moaned, and his hand shot unbidden to his ribs.

'What's wrong, Robby?'

'I ... I ....'

Go on, Robby told himself, the story's ready. Use it like Sean Wade used the hurley, like you used the unloaded rifle on McCabe. And missed, he thought.

'I had a bit of a smash in Eamon's car last night. Hurt my ribs.'

'Did you see a doctor?' O'Neill asked. Looking Robby up and down, he seemed to notice for the first time how dishevelled he was. 'You're wrecked, Robby. Where'd you sleep last night?'

'I didn't sleep. I couldn't. Eamon'll freak out when he sees the car. The radiator's in bits and I don't know what else. I sneaked it into the garage up at the yard,' Robby answered. His stomach tightened as if to receive a blow. 'I was going to ask you to have a look at it. But you can't leave Mam on her own.'

'No sweat, Robby. I'll ask Maisie McCarthy next door to come in for an hour or two. She'll be glad of a chance to snoop around. Nice woman, really, but nosy as hell.'

c03

When old men cry, they do it softly, having learned through bitter experience that no one is listening. Eamon's sobs were more pathetic still, Mayfly thought, because he knew he didn't deserve to be listened to. She was tired of watching him huddle in the gloom, his self-pitying helplessness spreading through her like a contagion. She held out little hope that McCabe would honour whatever bargain he'd made with Robby.

On her hands and knees, she crept across to Eamon. He was so absorbed in his own misery that he wasn't aware of her approach. She nudged his shoulder and he uncurled with a start. Then he looked up at her tearfully, mistaking her touch for the sympathy he craved.

'He'll never forgive me, will he?' he said. 'He'll never understand why I did the things I did.'

'Listen,' Mayfly said. 'Stop thinking about yourself for

five minutes, will you? There must be something we can do to get ourselves out of here.'

'What can we do, only wait for Robby to come back? There's no way out of this bloody —'

Mayfly gripped his arm. The inspiration came to her in a ferment of trepidation.

'Robby told me you made traps. Rat-traps, badger-traps,' she whispered. 'He said he dumped them in here whenever he found them in the fields.'

Both on their knees now, they could almost hear each other's thoughts leap forward.

'We could —' Mayfly began.

'Jesus, it'd be too risky, I don't —'

'We can't trust McCabe to ....'

'I know, I know. If we could snare —'

'... Before Robby got back —' she said.

They shifted the debris from the piles of junk slowly, carefully, like rescuers at the scene of a collapsed building. But it was their own survival they sought. When an old paint-can slipped from Eamon's grasp and clattered to the floor, they felt certain that McCabe would charge down from above. After a sickeningly tense interval, they resumed their task with even greater care, though their hands ached to hurry.

At last, Eamon came upon a saw-toothed steel badger-trap that, in other circumstances, would have appalled Mayfly. There was no time, however, for qualms of conscience.

'We can hide in the corner by the door,' she said quietly, 'and set the trap where he can't see it when he opens the door.'

Eamon shuffled ahead of her, cradling the trap in his arms. He placed it on the floor and began to unfold its jagged jaws. His hands shook as he squinted half-blindly at the deadly mechanism.

'It's too bloody dark. I can't see to set it.'

'You have to, Eamon.'

'If it snaps, it'll take my bloody hands off,' he groaned, straining to keep the great steel mouth open. 'I can't even remember how to set the bloody thing. It's so long since ... since I did anything at all.'

'Well, you'd better start now,' Mayfly said sharply, 'if you want to get out of this alive.'

'Why should I care?' Eamon muttered, the self-pity creeping back into his voice. 'Robby's all I've left, and you've heard what he thinks of me. He'll never —'

'What do you want, Eamon?' Mayfly snapped. 'You want to sit around here waiting for Robby to forgive you? Well, forget it, because it's not going to happen. Not unless you do something to get us all out of this. Set the trap.'

The trap was damp with Eamon's sweat when he'd finished. They eased back into the corner behind the door, fearing that their very breath might send the viciously pointed teeth crashing together.

೦೩

Speed was what Robby needed. A fast-moving car dulls the senses, stops you thinking, banishes second thoughts. O'Neill didn't oblige him. He was a careful driver at the best of times, and in his preoccupation he became even more cautious. As they crawled through the busy town square — it was Bingo night at the Premier Hall — he gave way to every last car that edged to join in the stream of traffic. The red Toyota Sprint purred longingly for a real revving-up, but O'Neill might as well have been at the wheel of Eamon's Cortina.

On the open road at last, they still didn't speak. The hand on the speedometer moved up to thirty-five, then to forty, and stayed there. Robby rolled and unrolled the seat-belt strap, moved his seat back and forward, opened and closed the window again and again. And it was working, all this nervy fidgeting, keeping his mind from what came next. Until the cemetery loomed ahead, the tall fingers of the pine trees beckoning.

His aching ribs shortened his breathing. What am I going to do, Sean? he thought. How the hell can I do right when all I have is a choice between two evils?

O'Neill touched the indicator and drew the car to a halt beside the cemetery gates.

'I thought we'd have a look at the grave,' he said, in answer to Robby's bewildered look. 'See what the damage is.'

The seat belt whisked upwards and he opened the driver's door. He glanced back at Robby.

'Are you sure you went to the doctor?' he asked.

Robby slumped forward, his head clasped between his hands. The bright starburst before his eyes swept inwards, seeming to split his brain into its component atoms. The ringing in his ears was the clamour of things falling apart.

'I ... I knocked down Sean's bloody cross. I drove the car into it. Why didn't it just fall on me?'

'It doesn't matter, Robby. Sean wouldn't have wanted a monument, anyway.'

'He wanted to be a martyr, didn't he? For Ireland only?'

'No, he didn't,' O'Neill said. 'He got angry, Robby, we all did. We made monsters of ourselves and we paid a price. Sean paid the heaviest price. I just had half my life stolen from me. And I'm still paying, Robby. Every day I'm trying to convince myself that what's happening to Grace isn't some punishment for my sins. There's fellows can put it all behind them, but I can't. Sean couldn't have either.'

The storm in Robby's head passed. He sat up and held his side. Tiredness pressed his shoulders down, and all the cramped tension of his muscles dissolved beneath its weight. He felt numb, but it wasn't the panicked numbness of his dream. The clenched fist that was his brain loosened as he spoke.

'Liam. McCabe is up at the house.'

The rest of it was easily and quickly told. O'Neill's astonishment was fleeting. He listened intently, and Robby began to believe that he was already hatching a rescue plan. The prospect of a final confrontation with McCabe, and of O'Neill using his old IRA experience to outwit him, had a galvanising effect on Robby. He felt certain that, for Mayfly's sake, he could fight through the pain one last time.

'There's only one way to deal with this,' O'Neill said, and Robby felt a surge of optimism. 'We'll have to go to the guards and —'

'What?' Robby exclaimed. 'We can't do that! He'll kill Mayfly. I know he will.'

'Look, Robby, forget this vigilante stuff. The guards know how to handle these situations.' O'Neill was looking in the rear-view mirror; it seemed to Robby he was too ashamed to look him in the eye. 'We'll get her out. If I have to go in there myself, we'll get them out. Look, when the guards come, don't tell them McCabe was looking for me. If it comes to it, I'll offer to go in and negotiate with him. He never psyched me out yet, he won't do it this ....'

O'Neill suddenly spun around in his seat. As he did, the pink and yellow dormobile flashed by on Robby's side of the car.

'He's come looking for Mayfly,' Robby cried. 'What are we going to —'

A white Ford Sierra swung out from the back road and blocked the dormobile's path. The screeching of brakes filled the air, and the dormobile lurched to a stop.

Then O'Neill's door shot open, and Detective Sergeant Healy was standing there. More cars were pulling up, and the Toyota was quickly surrounded by uniformed guards and armed plain-clothes men.

'Enjoy your trip to Dunmore South, did you, Robby?' Healy asked angrily.

'I was never in —'

'Don't lie, Robby. You're in deep enough as it is,' Healy snapped. 'We've a spy in the camp down there. Tipped us off this morning about "some young lad in a wreck of a Cortina" with a message for Mr Sharpe.'

'It's not his fault,' O'Neill said. 'He didn't let McCabe in. You know that.'

'Out of the car,' Healy began, but he was interrupted by a young guard who rushed to his side.

'There's a young one missing,' he said, pointing to the dormobile. 'That hippie fellow's daughter.'

Robby measured the space between the two vehicles and the ditch. If any sacrifices were going to be made, he was going to make them himself.

'She's in the house,' said O'Neill, getting out of the car and reaching back for the keys. In one movement, Robby knocked away his hand, jumped over to the driver's seat, and stamped on the accelerator. All around, bodies dived for cover and guns were raised threateningly as he steered the Toyota towards the dormobile, struggling desperately to close the door.

The ditch took the side-mirror on the passenger side. The high front bumper of the dormobile took the driver's door. Shots rang out and the back of the car swung wildly as a tyre exploded, near the farm entrance.

Robby abandoned the car by Eamon's wrecked Cortina, halfway along the lane. Crouching low, he made for the front of the house, under cover of the hedges.

He prayed he'd reach the cellar before McCabe, alerted by the gunfire on the road, got there first.

chapter 29

To Mayfly and Eamon, deep in the cellar, the shots sounded no louder than fingertips tapping lightly on a windowpane. McCabe's reaction to them, however, pounded in their ears, and their hearts raced as quickly as his approaching feet. The cellar air had thickened and grown more and more oppressive. Their clothes clung to them stickily as they crouched in readiness for McCabe's arrival.

The door was jerked open with such force that Mayfly was sure the trap would go off; but it held fast. The light blinded them momentarily, and Eamon gripped her arm protectively.

'Out! Out!' McCabe thundered, his shadow dancing maniacally on the junk-strewn floor. 'Where the hell ...?'

Mayfly tried to speak but her voice was a wordless whimper.

'I'm here,' Eamon croaked, and Mayfly didn't know if he was pretending to sound ill or really was.

'Out! Come on, out!' McCabe yelled. The barrel of the rifle appeared in the doorway, like a snake entering a pit.

'He can't move,' Mayfly said. 'Something's wrong. I think he's ....'

The shadow advanced. McCabe seemed suddenly so close that she was sure he'd stepped over the trap.

'He screwed me, Eamon. He —'

His scream was beyond all imagining, a scream from the very bowels of hell. The impact of the sprung trap sent him flying back to the doorway. Even as he fell, Mayfly and Eamon were charging towards the hallway.

As they passed McCabe, Mayfly saw that the rifle was still in his hand.

Eamon lurched ahead of her, leading the way through the kitchen, out into the yard and on towards the fields. With every step, Mayfly expected to hear gunfire and feel bullets sink into her back; but they reached the gate into the Stone Field. When they crawled through the bars they found themselves surrounded by dozens of policemen. In their midst stood Bubble, his arms held out to Mayfly, tears streaming down his face.

From all sides, more armed men approached. As Mayfly ran towards Bubble, she looked desperately among them for Robby.

'I thought I'd lost you, Fly,' Bubble cried, his face pressed to Mayfly's shoulder.

Up at the high circle of stones, a tall figure emerged. But it wasn't Robby, just another plainclothes policeman. A cramp of fear stiffened Mayfly's body, clutched at her throat. The question could find no passage from her brain to her parched lips.

Bubble answered it anyway, holding her tighter.

'He went back in for you, Fly,' he said.

Back at the gate, Eamon's cry rose and suddenly faded. The burly detective caught him before he fell.

ᔆ

The swaying trees were reflected in the tall windows of Cloghercree House like distant memories in reminiscing eyes. Robby dashed across the overgrown croquet lawn, almost tripping over a long-abandoned hoop buried in the grass. The windows hadn't been disturbed in years — except for one, near the gable end, which had a small block of wood inserted between the bottom timber and the sill. The frame came away in rotten lumps as Robby lifted, praying it wouldn't make a sound, hoping the scream he'd heard hadn't come from Eamon. For answer he got a low rumbling sound that might have passed for thunder.

The library he stood in contained no books, just rows of shelves buckling with dampness on walls of swollen plaster. A heavy oak door led to the empty room that had once been a study. Here, as a small child, loving the echoes in the place, Robby had sung the songs that Eamon surreptitiously taught him — *'don't be singing these in front of your mother.'* And a faint echo of that innocent singing lingered as he moved gingerly across to the door leading into the hallway.

'He died for Ireland and Ireland only,
The harp, the shamrock, green, white and ....'

Only when the door allowed a sliver of light into the hallway did he hear the low, gasping moan. Certain it was Eamon, Robby strained to sense some sign of Mayfly's presence, but found none. Silence wrapped itself like a shroud over the decaying house.

He peered into the hallway. He saw briefly that the cellar door, at the far end, was unlocked; but his attention was immediately seized by the sight on the stairs. A trail of dark blood, streaked and spotted, led upwards to the first landing.

Along by the wall he went, his soft-soled trainers taking him noiselessly across the tiles. The kitchen revealed nothing, nor did the view of the yard through the back door. Robby's heart raced as he stepped inside the cellar — but it was empty, except for the disturbed layers of broken, unwanted things. From the upper floor, the sounds of anguish resumed.

Robby's imagination was ablaze with wild speculations that, in his frantic state, seemed to him like certain truth. McCabe had shot Eamon and taken Mayfly away as a hostage ....

'Eamon!' he called. He ran to the stairs, bounding

upwards three, four steps at a time. 'Eamon ...!'

Half-hidden by the grandfather clock, McCabe sat against the wall, aiming the rifle shakily at Robby. The badger-trap was clamped to his left leg, just above the ankle, in a mess of blood and shorn denim. Sweat poured from him. He spoke through clenched teeth, his body heaving.

'Get this off me,' he gasped. 'The pain — uhhh — the pain .... I've a clear shot on you all the way down the stairs, boy, so don't ....'

Robby faltered on the second-to-last step to the landing. McCabe took his stumble for a prelude to escape and fired.

೮౩

The shot ringing out from the house was like a signal the policemen had been waiting for. Through the Stone Field gate they went, moving quickly, each one knowing exactly which position to take up in surrounding the bleak old building.

At first Mayfly froze, seized by a chilling dread. Then, with Bubble in her wake, she tried to follow them. At the gate, a dark-haired policewoman blocked their way.

'It's too dangerous down there,' she said. 'This fellow's liable to do anything.'

'You have to let me through! I have to ....'

'I'll keep her back from the house,' Bubble said. 'If we could just get into this field and see ....'

While Bubble pleaded with the young woman, Mayfly slipped past them and ran down the grassy slope she'd ascended only minutes before. Bubble and the police-woman called after her in alarm.

೮౩

Thick flakes of plaster continued to fall from the bullet-hole, as though the whole house was about to collapse

slowly in upon itself. Robby heard a faint echo of Mayfly's
name being called, and thought it came from within him.
He climbed to the landing and moved towards McCabe,
who was frantically checking the breach of the rifle.
Finding it empty, he threw it away and whipped out the
pistol from under his shirt.

'Move it, Robby,' he groaned, his eyes bulging with the
pressure of his pain. 'They're not going to get me like this,
caught like a bloody rat. Get it off me!'

Robby knelt beside him. He had no idea how the
spring-locks on Eamon's traps worked; he had always
refused to listen when his great-uncle tried to explain.

'It'll take time,' Robby said, a wave of nausea hitting
him as he saw the exposed bone through the tear in the
denim. 'And it'll hurt.'

'Just do it. Shut your bloody mouth and do it.'

His first touch of the trap would send McCabe into a
brain-splitting paroxysm of agony. Robby knew that
because he'd once tried to free a badger from that very
trap. He took a deep breath and located the pistol in the
corner of his eye as he reached down to the metal frame.

From downstairs came the sound of a door — the
kitchen door, Robby thought — being forced in.

'They're in the bloody house,' McCabe rasped. 'I'll
shoot you if you don't —'

In the same instant, Robby slammed one fist down on
the trap and the other into McCabe's pistol hand. As
McCabe screamed in agony, Robby lunged for the pistol,
but it cleared the landing and fell into the well of the
hallway. When it hit the hard tiles, a shot blasted from it
and hit the kitchen door, halting the advance of the people
inside.

But it didn't matter any more. Unarmed, there was
nothing McCabe could do to Robby. For a moment, Robby
thought McCabe had passed out; but those dark eyes had

only closed in upon themselves briefly, in a vain attempt to quell his suffering. He looked at Robby.

Robby started to laugh. He sank to his knees, and when he got there he was shaking his head, feeling drunk, feeling free.

'What's the big joke, you little bastard? Don't laugh at me, boy,' McCabe grunted. He tried to move forward but shrank back with a tormented grimace.

'The old reverse psychology, Razor,' Robby said. 'I was just thinking about the reverse psychology of all this. Think about it, Razor. Eamon, the man who broke his leg for Ireland — he just broke yours. Good one, hah? Hah?'

He was climbing to his feet, about to call out to his rescuers, when McCabe, with one last screaming effort, raised his right leg and kicked Robby in the hip. The woodwormy stair-rail gave way under Robby's clutching hand and he plunged down into the hallway, the hard tiles breaking his fall with a sickening, deadening jolt.

Distantly, he heard shots, more screams. He thought he heard Mayfly's scream above them all, but he couldn't be sure. He thought he saw her face floating ghostlike above him. But in the instant before the darkness finally fell, he knew that he himself was the ghost; because the words he read on her lips were, *'Sean, Sean, Sean!'*

# epilogue

Along the alleyway of tall pines in Cloghercree cemetery, their footsteps crackled through the still air of the summer afternoon. From the shade, they looked out at the sunlit harvest of gravestones. Up ahead, the stone crucifix on its high mound seemed magnified in the hazy heat. In their hearts, pangs of loss and hopes for the future vied for ascendancy like a moon and sun in the one sky.

A year had passed since that day of reckoning. In Mayfly's mind, the funerals were half-remembered events — hardly even recollections, more like accounts given to her by others. Though she'd been at them in body, her spirit had been elsewhere: away in some hidden fortress, deep in the forest of despair. No escape had seemed possible; nor had Mayfly, for a long time, even desired to escape.

Those had been days of quiet madness. Days spent talking to herself at Robby's bedside, trying to pretend he could hear her. Evenings spent trying to pretend that the new life Bubble planned for them in Cloghercree wasn't just another chapter of the same old story. Nights spent listening to Robby's tapes, trying to pretend that Jeff Buckley's voice was his and sang for her alone.

Mayfly was sure she couldn't have survived that dark passage if it hadn't been for Bubble. Just as he was walking beside her now in the cemetery, he'd walked beside her through those days. He had indulged her sorrowful apathy while, at the same time, gradually imposing some order on their lives.

When Robby's ailing great-uncle had offered them the

cottage to live in, Bubble had gone about its renovation with enthusiasm. Much later, he told Mayfly that the gift of the cottage had been the key to his own survival, and that he believed the unexpected offer was somehow meant to be. He and Andy had once promised each other that if one died, the other would end the journeying in that last place.

Bubble had two jobs: one helping out on the farm at Cloghercree, the other playing weekend gigs around the county. Neither he nor Mayfly ever mentioned the Sir Gordon alternative these days.

Because she had been too dispirited to protest, Mayfly had submitted to his suggestion that she start school in the nearby town. Very soon, the schoolwork had become a kind of anaesthetic. Lost in problems of maths and science and the like, she had found some respite from her inner tumult.

They turned left at the crucifix, the thick-branched evergreens still blocking out the sun. The imposing Celtic cross with its epitaph to Sean Wade was long gone. In its place stood a shiny black marble gravestone, hardly distinguishable from Andy's or from all the other stones around. It bore the names of, not one, but two Wades.

Out in the sunny clearing at last, Mayfly was glad of the warmth. She heard Robby's voice, always a miracle to her, each and every time she heard it. She turned to greet him.

଼

It wasn't easy, pushing a pram along this pebbled path. Each of the four wheels seemed to have a mind of its own. And then there was the little problem of picking up the rattle that six-month-old Shane made a habit of dropping every ten yards or so. Grace, walking a short distance behind with Liam O'Neill, had offered to take over, but Robby quite enjoyed his little brother's mischievousness. And, besides, he needed the distraction.

When he'd awoken from his coma at the hospital, he'd felt bombarded by the shocks that awaited him. Three months! He couldn't believe it. Nor could he quite believe that he'd survived with nothing worse than a fractured skull that was already almost healed. Mayfly had been there, with Grace, when he came to, and her presence seemed all the more extraordinary when he realised how much time had passed. Grace looked very tired, but with each passing minute she was renewed by sheer relief. Robby, too, had been hugely relieved to see her and to be assured that nothing had happened to the unborn child. For a while, that room had been all light and happiness.

And then had come the greatest shock of all. It couldn't have been easy for Liam to deliver the bad news, so soon after he'd arrived in a breathy rush, his face bright with delight at Robby's recovery.

They used to talk about people dying of a broken heart, Liam told Robby, and if it was ever true, it was true of Eamon. In spite of everything that had passed between them, his absence had left a gap in Robby's life as wide as that which Andy's absence left in Mayfly's. Somehow, the fact that McCabe had survived — though his sentence meant he would never leave prison again — deepened Robby's sense of loss. There was still much that he and Mayfly had to do to put their lives back together, though they'd come a long way.

The farm at Cloghercree was Robby's, and so was every penny of Eamon's savings — a sum that seemed astonishing to Robby, though he soon learned that money never went as far as you imagined it would. For months, he couldn't bring himself to go out to Cloghercree. He thought about selling the place to Mick Johnston. But, in the end, he had told Grace that he wanted to start up an organic farm.

He'd had a lot to learn; he still had. But, with Bubble's help and that of an organic farmer Liam knew, they'd put together a plan and were working hard to make a success of it.

Robby continued to live with Grace and Liam and his young brother. The house at Cloghercree remained empty. Sometimes Robby thought that someday he'd knock it down and build a new house there. But there were days, too, when he looked up from the his work in the fields and thought, *Maybe not, maybe not.*

Mayfly lifted the gurgling baby from his pram, and Robby walked alongside her as they wound their way, with the others, to Andy's grave. There they stood, as they'd done at Sean and Eamon's grave. Though the sun was shining, Robby was reminded of that overcast day when he'd returned to Cloghercree for the first time since his recovery. He'd stood below the stone circle with Mayfly. Neither of them had spoken. The stones had cast no shadows.

They felt the blessedness of spirits at rest. They felt the pulse of life in each other's hand.